The Work of Management

A Daily Path to Sustainable Improvement

by Jim Lancaster

with Emily Adams

Foreword by Jim Womack

Lean Enterprise Institute

ISBN 978-1-934109-02-1
Design by Thomas Skehan
Version 1.0

Lean Enterprise Institute, Inc.
215 First Street, Suite 300
Cambridge, MA 02142, USA
(t) 617-871-2900 • (f) 617-871-2999 • lean.org

Contents

Foreword
by Jim Womack

I am very excited about this book, in which Jim Lancaster tells the story of a 10-year journey at Lantech, the stretch-wrapper manufacturer in Louisville, Kentucky to install a lean management system and confirm its performance over an extended period. This is the inside view of the company as it proceeded from instability and an inability to sustain results of the kaizen work for which it was famous to a daily management system that creates stability for routine operations, sustains continuous improvement with A3 thinking, and facilitates big strategic leaps with hoshin planning while developing people at every level of the business.

In describing the journey, Jim demonstrates the key elements of daily management—a robust process involving every manager in every part of the business every day—as a flexible system able to deal with issues facing the business in real time. In plain language and illustrations, Jim shows a management system you can apply to your organization with dramatic results.

I first encountered Jim in 1994 when he was a young manager at Lantech, then at the end of a dramatic conversion of its production processes under the leadership of Pat Lancaster, Jim's father and the company's founder. It had been a remarkable effort to save the business by increasing velocity and shrinking lead times while reducing costs and improving quality, all by applying lean principles through high-speed kaizen. Lantech seemed to be a great story with a happy ending, and Dan Jones and I quickly decided to include it in *Lean Thinking*, where it became chapter 6.

I was so taken with Pat's success that I asked him to be on the LEI board when I founded the organization in 1997. He served for the next 15 years, which gave me the opportunity to keep track of Lantech's continuing adventures. In particular, Pat embraced strategy deployment (hoshin planning) and was proficient enough that I asked him to help me master these techniques at LEI as we started up.

Over the years, I visited Lantech on many occasions and gradually began to see a troubling pattern. The company was great at kaizen, trying new ideas with dramatic experiments, and often achieved dramatic short-term gains. It also pursued big strategic leaps through its annual hoshin process. But it was much less adept at sustaining the gains from kaizen or actually achieving hoshin breakthroughs. Indeed, I saw backsliding to preexisting performance levels after bold leaps. This pattern was particularly interesting to me because it was becoming evident all across the lean community.

As this trend emerged, Pat was thinking about the transition to the next generation, and Jim was being groomed to take over as CEO. Jim will tell his own story in the pages ahead of what happened after he became CEO in 1995, but let me explain here that Lantech then employed what I call *entrepreneurial*, or *traditional*, *management*. Pat, the founder, was (and still is) a brilliant inventor who had gathered a group of colleagues who could execute on his vision for a new company in a new industry. Little formal management was needed. The team knew what Pat wanted, and they worked hard to achieve it. No detailed measures of performance and no complex means for dealing with cross-functional issues were needed. The next new thing was always the focus of the team, not steady-state management of the growing and maturing business Lantech was becoming.

When Jim stepped up to be CEO, he brought along a very different approach to management. He hired a new president of the North American business unit who assigned objective performance measures to the work of subordinates and held them accountable for making their numbers. Longevity of service in the organization and loyalty to the founder were not the point. Results were. This is the familiar large-enterprise approach to management by results rather than management by process that I call *modern management*.

Soon into his tenure as CEO, Jim realized that the replacement of traditional with modern management was not working. Managers were bewildered and offended by the new system. Some rebelled and others quit. And most important, performance of the business did not improve.

Fortunately, Jim found a coach for his management issues, just as Pat had found one years earlier for his process issues. Jim's coach was Bob Morgan, whom I had met in 1993 even before I happened across Lantech. Bob was then the general manager of a steering-gear business in Wales in the United Kingdom that supplied both Toyota and Honda. He had been an early convert to lean thinking, but unlike many other managers at this time, he had focused on the management elements of the system, rather than just the process elements. He had balanced the social and the technical elements in a creative way. When I founded LEI a few years later, I was so impressed with what he had done in several companies where he subsequently worked as a senior manager that I also asked him to join the board.

Soon I noticed Pat and Bob were talking on the side at board meetings about the problems with the management transition at Lantech. This book is the story of what happened when Bob Morgan began to coach Jim Lancaster.

Through a series of experiments, Jim created a lean management system that could create and sustain stability in the performance of every value-creating process at Lantech. This daily approach to management has become the firm foundation for sustainable improvement through kaizen and successful hoshin planning. It was a new way to think creatively about what Jim calls "the real work of management."

This book is therefore two things at once. On one level, it is a second Lantech story, also with a happy ending, this time proved to be sustainable over many years. I think you will find it inspiring and fun too. On a deeper level, it describes a method you can use to create your own lean management system in any type of business based on daily and weekly management for stable performance. This becomes the foundation for sustainable kaizen through A3 thinking, and successful big initiatives through hoshin planning—all done to the steady cadence of a daily and weekly management cycle.

It has been a great honor to share the confidence of Pat, Jim, and Bob over many years, often at times when they were struggling to find the way ahead. I have seen them face and solve one business problem after another, evolving from a small lean startup founded on a brilliant product innovation, to scaling up with efficiency and quality via lean production, to creating stability via a lean management system. Through their experiments I have learned much of what I know about lean management, and I am grateful they have agreed with our suggestion at LEI that they now share their learning and wisdom with you.

As always with LEI publications, we (and Jim) would love to hear from you about your experiments and results—good and bad. Simply contact us at info@lean.org. With some courage (which you must supply) and a lot of experiments (as described in these pages), we are confident that you and your organization can also master the work of management.

Jim Womack
Founder and Senior Advisor
Lean Enterprise Institute
Barters Island, Maine
January 2017

This book is dedicated to the employees of Lantech, who show up every morning ready to work. Without their dedication and patience—their willingness to work alongside us as we all tried and failed at this system and then tried and failed and tried again—we never could have found the success and stability that we enjoy today.

– Jim

Chapter 1

Stumbling

I f I had only one word to describe myself as a CEO in the early 2000s, it would have been *frustrated*. If you had seen me standing there applauding the efforts of another cross-functional improvement team, you might not have known it. But I was.

My company was famous as a pioneer of continuous improvement, so my feelings were a kind of heresy. But I could not fail to see the problems on my plant floor, where I could watch a *kaizen*[1] team working with focused intensity to improve the manufacturing process of one product, trying to correct and perfect every bit of work, while another work area nearby completely fell apart. Most likely that area would contain a very expensive custom machine that was full of engineering errors and $10,000 worth of structural rework, but no kaizen team would be working on the cause of this machine's very immediate problems. It seemed like I was always calling an angry customer to explain and apologize.

On one day in particular, I remember standing there watching some similar scenario play out—striving for excellence in one area while last year's fully improved and kaizened area fell apart, wondering why all of our problems came back—when a tour group

---

1. From the Japanese characters for "change" and "good," *kaizen* is defined as continuous improvement of an entire value stream or an individual process to create more value with less waste.

came through. This happened a lot in those days. One of our continuous-improvement engineers was leading around a group of visiting engineers and executives, pointing out the lean features of our world-class manufacturing facility. I sighed and trudged up the stairs to attend another improvement team's report-out.

Sure, we all liked the attention and the praise, but I knew we had some fundamental problems and one very big secret. Lantech, the smart and enthusiastic company featured in the seminal book *Lean Thinking*,[2] was not delivering great business results. We were working hard. We were conducting multiple kaizen workshops every month, diligently removing waste from the system and continuously improving. Every week, teams reported savings of time and money, but it all seemed to evaporate before it could hit the income statement. How had we wound up here? Just a bit of history helps explain.

My dad, Pat Lancaster, started this company in 1972 with his brother, Bill, and it was a classic American success story. Pat had a good idea for building a machine that would secure a load of boxes, containers, or bags on a pallet for shipping. Instead of shrink-wrapping the pallet and load, he made a machine that wrapped the whole thing in plastic film. He called it stretch wrap. His method used less than half of the plastic per load and avoided the extra, expensive heating-step of a shrink wrapper.

Pat found good employees in our native Louisville, KY— local craftspeople who could read a set of blueprints and build from them. Then, he listened to his customers, watched how they used the equipment, and kept innovating. If a Lantech machine had a problem, we always showed up to fix it. We were known for our loyalty to customers and for product innovation.

---

2. James P. Womack and Daniel T. Jones, *Lean Thinking: Banish Waste and Create Wealth in Your Corporation*, 2nd ed., (New York: Simon and Schuster, 2003).

I had worked at Lantech since I was kid, sweeping floors, folding blueprints, learning to assemble machines. I had personally cleaned the bugs out of every lighting fixture in the building. But I had been away for several years, in school and working, when my dad lured me back from New York City in 1990. I liked working in finance and living in the big city, but I could not turn away from Lantech and Louisville. They were home. They were where I wanted to bring my new bride and raise a family.

The trouble was Lantech was in a lot of debt and struggling. We had just lost the protection of a critical patent (in a travesty of justice). My dad was working harder than ever, but the shop floor was drowning in inventory, and nearly every machine shipped out later than promised.

Great ideas from the past were killing us. The plant was filled with batches of machine modules that previous forecasts said we would need; the MRP system ensured we had lots of parts, just not the ones we needed. It took 14 weeks to build and deliver even a simple machine, which was why we built to stock. And valuable new product ideas lay dormant because our resources were absorbed in getting problem machines shipped.

Pat knew that he and his company needed to change. In the early 1990s, my dad learned about the ideas of the Toyota Production System and what would come to be called *lean* and embraced them with gusto. He hired a new director of operations, Ron Hicks, and he helped us remake operations. Working together in teams of people from throughout the company, assisted by a newly created group of lean experts in a Kaizen Promotion Office, we got rid of the old batch-and-queue methods and embraced one-piece flow.

The inventory evaporated. Within a few years we went from two inventory turns annually to 11, freeing up more than $3 million in cash. The debt was paid off. Manufacturing lead time on some machines dropped from 14 weeks to 8 hours. It is difficult to overstate the revolution that Lantech was experiencing.

In those early years, in the 1990s, I was on the road a lot, selling our machines and building the distribution network. I was a little jealous of Ron and Pat back in Louisville and the energy and excitement they were creating. Every time I came back into the plant, it seemed like it was a little cleaner and a lot easier to see how things actually got built. Lantech soon became a model lean enterprise, hosting public kaizen workshops where outsiders learned about lean and what we had accomplished while working on teams to solve our production issues.

By 1995 when I took over as CEO and my dad happily "retired" to our product-development efforts, we had freed something like 60 people from their old production and office jobs, and a lot of them joined Pat in product development. We had greatly expanded our distribution channel to absorb some of the capacity we had created. Then Jim Womack and Dan Jones came to visit. They featured Lantech in an article in the *Harvard Business Review*[3] and then, shortly afterward, published their book that sparked a new definition of excellence. We were famous.

Working closely with Ron and Jean Cunningham, our CFO, we took lean thinking through our offices too. I described it as a kaizen blitz. We slashed the amount of time it took to enter an order from two weeks to just hours. Jean made so many improvements to the finance department—including slashing the amount of time it took to close the books every month to a single day— that she wrote a book about it with another lean CFO.[4]

---

3. James P. Womack and Daniel T. Jones, "Beyond Toyota: How to Root out Waste and Pursue Perfection," *Harvard Business Review* (September–October 1996).
4. Jean E. Cunningham and Orest J. Fiume, *Real Numbers: Management Accounting in a Lean Organization* (Durham, NC: Managing Times Press, 2003).

Now, it was time to make my mark. Better production was great, but the financial benefits were becoming fewer and smaller. I decided it was time to expand Lantech by acquiring companies with similar product lines. In the late 1990s, Ron, Jean, and I went flying around the world, looking at acquisition candidates, thinking about how lean methods would remake each one.

In a ratty old barn in the middle of California, for instance, Jean and I visited a factory where they made the case-erector machines that automatically fold up the cardboard trays to hold fruit or nuts or vegetables. It was dirty. The barn smelled like sweaty old shoes, and their production methods were appalling— something like Lantech was doing 10 or 15 years earlier. So when we looked at their books, I was surprised to see they were showing profit of 12%–13% of gross revenue.

Back on the plane, I turned to Jean and asked how come we had people writing books about how good we were when our financial results were still just stubbornly average? We were not losing money, but we were averaging only 5% profit of gross revenue on our best years. We shook our heads over it, but neither of us had an answer.

In the Deep South a couple of weeks later, at the end of a long gravel road, I was in a factory that made conveyors. The owner was hoping to retire and spend more time squirrel hunting, so he was happy to show me around. Again, I found mountains of inventory and spare parts, a classic push system that acted without regard for the customer, and they were making 10% on gross income and had more than $10 million in cash.

With our capabilities, Lantech should have been in the top quartile of the capital-equipment industry in terms of financial performance. We should have had double-digit revenue growth and made at least 10% bottom-line profit as a percentage of gross revenue and even more EBIDA.[5] Since we had a profit-sharing bonus program with our employees, everyone had a keen interest in our revenue and profit performance. But Lantech was realizing half its potential even while becoming famous as a powerhouse of lean production methods.

I would pose this dilemma—*If we're so good, how come we aren't leading the industry financially?*—to my executive team and get the same responses every time. Operations would say that we couldn't fully standardize and stabilize the process until we stopped changing the product so much. Service would complain that operations was sending out so many quality problems that they could not keep up with the field-fix demand. Sales would agree that we were making a lot of customers angry, requiring us to discount machines to keep customers. Pat in product development (aka my dad) would say his team had great new ideas and if we could just start building machines incorporating them, customers would be thrilled and demand would grow with good margins.

I was stuck. I knew it was wrong to let the department heads all point angry fingers at each other, but I couldn't stop it. Everyone's argument made sense. I did not know how to get out of the trap.

A few months went by as I clapped politely for kaizen team reports, wondering where all of those improvements went, and studied new acquisition targets. We bought a struggling shrink-wrapper equipment company in Florida and a case-erector equipment maker in the Netherlands.[6] We went to work on converting the Dutch company to one-piece flow[7] and moving the shrink-

---

5. EBIDA: earning before interest, depreciation, and amortization.
6. A case erector folds up flat pieces of preprinted cardboard to create boxes or trays in which product is stacked.
7. One-piece flow in assembly means lining up all of the process steps in tight sequence and assembling machines (product) as they move from station to station with no machines waiting between stations.

wrapper operation to Kentucky. And then, like most equipment manufacturers, we got hit hard by the recession of 2001, and sales dropped by 14%. I could see even our slim margins slipping and decided it was time to refocus on the shop floor.

In the next year, I struggled to get everyone focused again on production, finding waste, improving operations, and using resources freed up by the drop in demand. But we all seemed to be going in different directions. In the downturn, I should have been able to use our people who were unneeded on the production line (excess resources) to drive faster improvement, thereby justifying overcapacity by increasing the company's long-term capability and keeping all our folks employed. But after a year of trying, I saw little result and ended up laying off about 10% of our employees to rebalance production resources with reduced demand. It was a horrible, emotional experience that drove many of my decisions in the coming years.

In 2004, Ron and Jean left. And I ended up in Cincinnati, in Bob Morgan's living room, trying to pique his interest in Lantech.

For a number of years, Pat had served with Bob on the board of directors of the Lean Enterprise Institute, and we knew him as a thoughtful man of good, solid advice. A former senior manager in large automotive supplier companies, Bob was one of those rare folks who had led multiple lean transformations. Most people just talk. Bob had experience and was known for a deep understanding of lean principles and, most importantly, the ability to make the work come to life in real companies. I was sure he could turn around our record of disappearing improvements and stagnant earnings.

Bob turned me down flat when I offered him a job. However, he took pity on me and spent an hour or two talking about what was going wrong in my business. He had interesting questions and good suggestions, but in the end, I went back to Louisville alone.

Next, I turned for advice to a group of fellow business leaders I had learned to value for the diversity of their experience. I was inclined to agree when they told me, "Jim, you need to get a strong manager in there to help. You are a really nice guy, and you're just not holding people accountable. You need to be focused on higher-level acquisition activities, and a strong manager is what you need, a person who will create an accountability culture."

So, I hired a new CFO and a very experienced, results-driven leader as president of North American operations and let them run things their way. I thought maybe these new people could find a way to drive improvement to the bottom line.

The culture shock was huge and nearly did us in. The new president managed operations by hammering out agreements with operations leaders about what would be accomplished in the next week, month, and year. He did this without fully understanding those operations or what was actually possible. When those leaders failed to meet objectives, they were labeled as failures—sometimes in front of large groups of people. I lost good people in that year as I allowed the experiment to play out.

And then I went back to Cincinnati, to Bob Morgan's living room, where I was lucky to catch him. Bob had retired from Delphi Automotive and was selling his house to set in motion his plans to leave the United States (he is British) and retire to his sailing yacht. He listened again to my tale of woe. Only this time, he said he might be willing to help me. He could not join us full-time, but he thought I was prepared to finally see and fix my problems, and he was prepared to mentor me.

Bob directed me to Mexico, to an automotive air-conditioning component plant that he had overseen while at Delphi.[8] He flew in from his boat to meet me, and when we went out to the floor

---

8. Bob Morgan was vice president of operations in the climate controls sector of Delphi, with responsibility for transforming a number of large plants around the world.

together, I saw the production lines clicking along. Everything was clean and orderly and simply … running. Then we went to a series of stand-up management meetings and that's where my jaw dropped.

Here were engineers, product managers, and maintenance and operations people talking about issues and performance abnormalities from the line that morning. They even had parts in their hands to talk about specific problems, and they were deciding right there what they were going to do. Operators and area supervisors had brought some of the issues to their attention. Other issues were on the managers' own tick lists. But here is what's important: they were not bickering and finger-pointing; they were talking about how to address those issues during the remainder of the day and who would be responsible for getting it done.

At Lantech, someone might complain about a problem to their manager, who might pass it along to their manager or put it up on large flip charts we had in each area. We called them barrier boards. This was where problems accumulated. Managers met once a week at the barrier boards to analyze the problems and decide which were the most important. We had meetings where we would look at 50 problems and argue about which were really important and then assign someone to get data so we could determine which of the really important problems were most important. Then, we could finally decide at a subsequent meeting what to do, and assign it to someone who would assemble a team, and meanwhile, we might be weeks later.

We were talking about what to do and deciding what to do and not actually doing all that much. What I saw in Mexico was managers responding immediately to anything that got in the way of an operator making a quality part safely, on time, and at cost.

The Mexican plant was one that Bob had transformed using professionals from Toyota and Delphi's own internal improvement teams and then used as a model factory to train other managers.

They introduced one-piece flow and conducted root-cause analysis and the plan-do-check-act (PDCA) method of problem solving. Everything was clean and in its place. They had a robust production system focused on customer pull, and they empowered people to find and solve problems, often the same day.

The difference was management *at every level* was actually involved in operational issues on a daily—even an hourly—basis. They had a two-hour series of interlocking *gemba*[9] walks and stand-up meetings in each area, with updates every morning on the resolution of problems encountered the previous day. At the end of those two hours, every person in the management team was updated on every aspect of operations needed to support the frontline work. That was everyone's job: supporting the frontline work, the value-creating activity of the company.

This ability to resolve frontline problems immediately was the piece we were missing at Lantech. For all of our amazing production breakthroughs, we had never stabilized our value-creating processes. But here was a system where all the brains of an organization were systematically focused on solving immediate operational issues without emotional scenes.

I knew from our kaizen experiences in the 1990s that when we really focused in on the work, the effort was repaid in multiples. Moving to one-piece flow saved our business because we achieved control—even temporarily—over how we made things. We lost that control when we looked up from the work and focused too much on other things. With a daily management system, focusing on the work in every department would become part of everyone's day.

---

9. The Japanese term for "actual place," often used for the shop floor or any place where value-creating work actually gets done.

Fundamentally it felt right. Bob agreed to work with us in Louisville, but only for a couple of days each month. He warned me that he would not be telling anyone what to do. His job would be to teach us how to see and think about work, and how to organize ourselves to enable value creation by frontline associates. In short, he would teach us how to manage work. He would give workshops and assign homework. The rest would be up to us.

Also, he said my presence and active participation were required if he was going to help. In truth, I had not spent much time on the shop floor since I was a teenager. Lately, I had spent a lot of time with our recent acquisitions and was letting the new executive team have all the space they needed.

I asked Bob who would do my job while I was down on the shop floor. He said, "What job? You mean, going to all those meetings you say are useless? Taking care of a planning process that does not get executed?"

I asked Gina McIntosh, who was then the team leader for manufacturing and is now director of operations, to keep an eye on things in the office while I got to work.

There was an awful lot of mess and waste on that shop floor. It was disappointing, considering all of the work we had done in the 1990s to clean it up. But the sight of that low-hanging fruit energized me, too, as we started to fix things.

I invited our president of North American operations and the CFO to join me, along with Steve Clifford, the manager of our lean transformation team, when Bob delivered his first workshop on standardized work in 2006. Of course, we thought we had been doing standardized work for more than 10 years at this point. It was humbling to realize that I had never understood the full nature of this concept, but I had little time to be embarrassed. We were going out on the shop floor, I told the president and the CFO, to find out what was really happening there.

We began with the feeder cells for the S-Auto, our automatic stretch-wrapping machine. The feeder cells make the modules that are assembled together to make an S-Auto. These include the electrical panel, the safety gates, the film delivery system, the big wrap arm—which sends the film delivery system speeding around a load of goods on a pallet, wrapping it up tight—and the automation module. It's probably not important that you know exactly how these modules interact, but we needed to know everything about how these pieces get made. We chose this area because the feeder cells had both downstream customers and upstream suppliers and because quality issues made the S-Auto both a critical business problem and an opportunity.

Bob set up a table in the middle of the area, gave us some instruction on how to characterize what was going on, and then sent us into the feeder cells with pencils and paper to sketch the work. Every day, I showed up at 6 a.m. in my steel-toed boots and went directly into the cells to sketch and look for work flows that were hard and tedious for the operators.

We were conscious of being respectful to the people working in the cells and tried to stay out of their way as we drew tools, hands, workbenches, and components. We drew arrows between steps to show the order and flow of work as it happened. And then Bob came around and pointed out our errors. He would ask, "Where did this tool come from? What was the missing step between these two processes? How did the materials and tools interact with the hands of the associates?"

Sketching forced us to both observe the work and translate it onto the page. On paper we learned to see the gaps—the missing pieces of work that we had not noticed—and then go back and look at the work process again. Filling in the gaps forced us to see and consider all the little bits of activity that make up the whole of a work process. We could not begin to improve, Bob taught us, until we really saw.

After we sketched the process, we improved it. Then we standardized the process, making it easily repeatable within the available time, and stayed there fixing issues until the process was completely stable and producing a good result every time. We were used to creating work processes that were significant improvements upon the former processes. Now, these needed to be improved, reexamined, and perfected. It was hard work but exciting too. When I got back to my office at 3 p.m. every day to deal with the mountain of other issues, I felt as though I understood my company better.

Detail of a Sketch from the Paint Line Observations

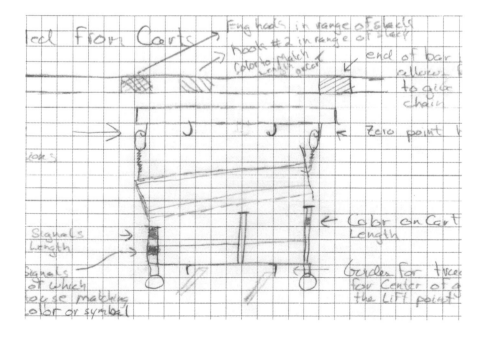

A few weeks later, Bob would come back and go directly to the area where we had been working to observe our improvements. Inevitably, something would be askew. There might be extra work-in-progress (WIP) on a bench or people wandering around looking for information or missing parts.

We would say, "Well, today isn't a normal day because ..."

Whatever our excuse, Bob would tell us to go back in and find out what was wrong and fix it.

"Today is perfectly normal," he told us. "It is normal because something unusual is always happening."

After a couple of months of this, we began looking forward to our next topic on Bob's learning tour—a workshop to teach us how to set up frontline management. We would schedule this workshop. Then Bob would arrive on the appointed date, go to our "improved" feeder cells, point out the instability, and cancel the new workshop in favor of fixing the feeder cells. He'd say that we could not move on until we really understood and could design good work. It was like failing first grade over and over again, and that went on for months.

My new executives were not happy—especially the president of North American operations. He wanted to debate this path we were on. A lot. He argued that there was little value in spending his very expensive time on something that a $12-an-hour operator could be doing. I took his point. After all, I had good leaders who had risen through the ranks and were really interested in the way that work gets done. It turned out that his time really was too expensive. Within about six months he exited our company. I got back to work.

That was later in 2006. What I learned in the years that followed—from Bob Morgan, the Lantech shop floor, and the people who work there—is that it is a chaotic world we live in. Parts supply and quality are unstable. Employees and customers can be unsteady. Tools are unreliable. We spend a lot of time trying to organize the elements just enough every day so that products get shipped, people stay safe, and money gets made. We do this with our daily management system (which I will describe in detail in the next chapter).

Bob says that keeping operations running smoothly is like maintaining a sand castle. If you keep after it every day—adding a little more sand here, a little water there, shoring up a support wall—you keep it intact. Turn your back and let the waves have their way and you have to build it all over again.

Working with our daily management system, I have learned that instability acts like a gravitational force, but management can organize itself to consistently make the right corrections. Doing so creates a different kind of stability—one that is not stiff and unbending but flexible and responsive to today's demands.

For us, this management system and the principles behind it have made a big difference. Production processes today are far more controlled. The majority of problems get solved when they are still small. We can see deterioration of a process very quickly and hold it back, allowing improvements to stick and then accumulate so that we actually affect financial performance.

At the end of 2007, we put the skeleton of the management system in place in a single week. In that first year we focused only on quality, taking baby steps with our new way of managing. Still, we saw number of defects per machine drop 70%–90% in most areas.

In the second year, as the Great Recession rolled across the country, we added cost measures to the mix and dramatically lowered monthly expenses while improving our gross margin. Like most companies in our industry, we had a significant revenue drop, but we were able to maintain profitability.

In the years that followed, we steadily deepened our commitment to the system and learned that the stability it created permitted us to sustain our kaizen efforts as never before and to tackle strategic initiatives that we could never have hoped to succeed with before.

I do not want this to sound like magic. Too many books about business improvements seem to promise some kind of fairy dust that will make profits soar. A daily management system, by definition, requires daily attention and dogged discipline. As a pilot—flying planes is what I love to do when I am not tending to my business—I know the value of ingrained habits such as checklists. That's what this management system feels like to me: a good and useful habit.

To those leaders who are willing to show up every day, who are committed to a morning management routine and to supporting those people who are doing the value-creating work of the company, this system will be a revelation. It will take 60 or 90 minutes out of your morning, but those will end up being the most important minutes of the day. And you will soon have more rather than less time available for activities focused on improving and expanding your business.

Chapter 2

Paint Line Team Leader for Life

Bob was not talking to me about a comprehensive daily management system when I went to work on the paint line in 2007. He told me that the job of management is to maintain working conditions before trying to improve them. But we could not truly *maintain* working conditions until standardized work was in place and processes were stabilized. He expected us to be working very hard at Lantech for a very long time just to maintain current performance. We selected the paint line as my first assignment due to the number of seemingly intractable problems there.

First, I taught a small team to understand the current work by watching and sketching all the work. Then, we created the standardized work necessary to maintain the current work. Our goal was a stable process[10] with the same performance day after day. I had no idea how difficult that would be.

I gathered a cross-functional team of about 10 Lantech associates from various levels and areas of expertise, taught them what I knew about observation and standardized work, and split them up into two-person teams to find out everything we could about our powder-coat painting process. In our Louisville plant,

---

10. We define a stable process as one that produces consistent quality and quantity within the same elapsed time, without unusual interventions, and that can be performed by many different associates (not a single heroic one).

the paint line is a monument in the center of the building, responsible for powder-coating every metal frame and part that we make for every machine a vibrant Lantech blue.

To give a clearer picture of our business, I should say here that Lantech is a make-to-order company. No parts or machines are produced without a customer order. As orders are finalized, we build a production schedule that includes making or buying every component and then assembling the complete machine. Painting metal parts is just one of the many tasks that must be accomplished in the right order, at the right time to produce machines on time and without leaving people idle. While many of our work cells dedicated to activities such as frame welding, final assembly, creating electrical panels, and making conveyors are designed to be flexible with regard to the precise items made and the production rates, the paint line is a large, unmovable monument.

On a day when everything was working to schedule, all the to-be-painted parts for a Q-Semi machine—our most popular turntable stretch wrapper—arrived at the paint line on a roller carriage every 54 minutes. The parts for an S-Auto, which secures loads from an overhead stretch-film dispenser and is far larger, would show up for paint every three hours. Parts for conveyor sections appeared every 20 minutes. Every work cell downstream from the paint line was accustomed to a certain amount of downtime in the day as operators waited for parts to be painted. In the past, we tried to fill the downtime with chores such as cleaning (5S). Now we were going to try to understand the paint process and eliminate the downtime.

We split up the work, with two-person teams each watching one of the paint line's four major workstations: loading/unloading, wash, dry-and-prep for paint, and operating the spray gun inside the paint booth itself. We saw a lot of examples of work that was difficult and tedious. Loading heavy frames onto the overhead conveyor hooks was a safety nightmare. The conveyor was too high to easily grab by at least 10 inches. So a forklift would move forward and lift a piece to the right height so a person on a stepladder could maneuver a support chain onto the overhead hook. Then the forklift would back up, the loader would hook a couple of lighter-weight pieces onto the conveyor, and then the forklift would be back with a big welded frame.

In short, we had a person on a forklift simply moving backward and forward for hours. And part of this tedious, mind-numbing job was to drive the forklift straight at a coworker standing on a ladder. We were begging for an accident. As I watched, the driver sometimes moved backward and forward a few feet for no reason. Just to stay occupied, most likely.

In the dry-and-prep area, we watched as operators plugged holes and covered areas such as screw threads that should not be painted. It was a haphazard process. They might be looking at the same frame piece—same drilled holes, same screw threads—five times a day, but each time they came at it differently, as if they had never seen it before.

I could see why every assembly cell downstream of the paint line had sandpaper and spray paint on hand to touch up mistakes. But every mistake is just an opportunity, right?

Our biggest revelation on the paint line, though, was that it was not operating to serve the needs of the assembly cells immediately downstream. Even small problems in fabrication areas upstream from paint—such as a welder late for work—meant that parts might arrive out of sequence for downstream needs. The associates on the paint line then had no guidance on which parts took priority in order to keep downstream areas working as smoothly as possible. One assembly cell could be stalled and waiting for painted parts while the paint booth was busy painting parts for other assembly cells not yet ready for more parts simply because these parts had arrived at paint early and cut in line in front of the parts we actually needed. The repercussions were always rippling far and wide.

So we took out our lean tools. We lowered the loading section of the overhead conveyor by several inches, nearly eliminating the need for a forklift for the loading task. We calculated takt times and created a sequence for the paint line based on the knowledge that the assembly cells working to takt time to meet customer demand would need, for instance, a conveyor every 20 minutes and the frame for a Q-Semi every 54 minutes.

The sequence also had a few blank slots for unforeseen work as we tried to respond to the real world of our production environment. For example, production rates for conveyors and frames might change every week based on adjustments to the overall production schedule at the start of fabrication. The point was for the paint booth to stick as close to the sequence as possible and hang parts only when there was an order card from assembly. This standardized the decision of what parts to hang next on the line.

If the overall production sequence and all of our operations were working perfectly, of course, we would not need a separate sequencer for the paint line. But we kept falling just short of perfection. We needed the paint sequence to reestablish an even flow of parts to the rest of the work cells. Also, this sequence helped make it immediately clear to the paint line team leader whether operations were on track. A glance at the sequence would tell them whether the parts in the loading area matched what was needed next in the downstream work cells. If they didn't match, the paint team leader could check with the upstream and downstream processes and make an informed decision whether to wait or let other pieces jump the line.

In the dry-and-prep area, we standardized the formerly random hole-plugging task so that when an operator is looking at the left side of a Q-Semi, for instance, they would know by the standard work that six plugs were needed. They would reach into the pocketed tool apron we gave them, pull out six plugs, and—working left to right and top to bottom—would plug the six holes. If they had one left over in their hand, it meant they missed a hole. It was a revelation. In just a few weeks, we took those spray paint cans away from all the downstream operations. If touch-ups were needed, people turned on andon lights that called the paint-line team leader over to investigate and solve the problem.[11]

I hope it does not sound like every idea we had worked right the first time. In fact, that was rarely the case. One of the most important lessons I learned in this process was to stick with it, working through the incomplete ideas and the solutions with bad repercussions. Eventually, good ideas take hold but usually only after working through many almost-good ideas.

By summer 2007 the paint line was not perfect, but its output was stable. It was safer for operators and was delivering painted parts out to the assembly areas as they were needed. For a few more weeks, I visited the area daily, checking in with the team leader and helping to talk through and solve small issues. Three months after we started sketching the work processes there, I saw an end to my days on the paint line and turned again to the rest of my business. I had neglected our European operation, which was scheduled for a strategic planning session. So I got on a plane and threw myself into planning with the team in the Netherlands for about two weeks. And that was all it took.

---

11. These days, paint touch-ups are done only at final inspection, right before a machine is crated for shipping. The number and nature of scratches or smears needing touch-ups are noted for corrective action upstream.

When I returned to work in Louisville, I went first to the paint area. I will admit I was excited to see it again. I liked the people on the line and thought we could bask in a job well done. I did not put on my steel-toed shoes because I was just checking in.

The first thing I saw was that they were obviously painting whatever showed up. They were not using the sequencer that we had set up, and there was a pileup of parts at loading. I went back to the dry-and-prep area. The operator was not wearing his apron or counting out plugs into his hand. And inside the paint booth, they were just willy-nilly painting parts—not using the top-down, left-to-right method for complete coverage.

I probably cussed out loud.

When I confronted the team leader (in the nicest way possible), he all but shrugged at me. In my experience, most front-line managers don't believe they can really standardize the work of operators. The person with their hand on the tool is just going to do it the way they want to do it, supervisors have told me. So, we are already running at a disadvantage when we try to implement a stable, standardized system.

But this team leader had another issue, too. "The day after you left, we got a huge influx of special-color paint jobs and non-standard modules," he told me. "So I worked them in. But then the schedule got all messed up."

We had not planned for big surges of work, and the team lost its rhythm. The careful, synchronized plan fell apart that second day, and they never recovered it. The new way was not a habit, so it was easier to just do it the old way.

I stayed out there for half a day, and we got the sequencer going again, got the dry-and-prep operator back into his apron, and got the paint gun moving methodically over parts. Then I went upstairs and tried not to shout at anyone.

Two weeks later, Bob was back to run another workshop, and I told him the story. "I'm frustrated," I said. "Do I have to be paint line team leader for life just to make sure our work stays in place?"

Bob looked at me over the top of his reading glasses and broke into the broadest grin I had ever seen on him. "You're ready," he said.

We went into my office, and he told me that my experience on the paint line had been necessary to prepare me for the next phase. He started sketching on my whiteboard and talking over his shoulder, saying that this next phase was the only way he knew how to truly stabilize and maintain frontline work.

Bob drew a map of the whole plant and then paths through it with triangles and squares and people's names and functions, all in a flurry. This was the map of the daily management system, a systematic review process in every work area, from the bottom to the top of our organization, that would help us grasp the actual work that was happening today and stabilize it—so long as we committed to doing it every day (*see an early iteration on page 24*). It would require that every manager and executive at Lantech adopt some standardized work into their day. For example, a front line team leader might have 55% of their day guided by standardized work, while the director of manufacturing might be at 35%. And I would have 5%–10% of my time spent at standardized work.

Each level's standardized work would loop through the work of the managers above and below, creating a continuous flow of information so that everyone would know the conditions at the front line and could support the work there. It sounded complicated, but I trusted Bob to steer me right.

Map of Early Daily Management System—Top Level

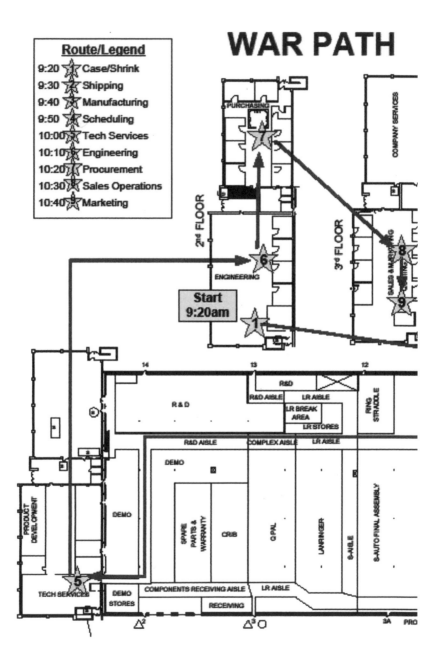

M-Th Loop

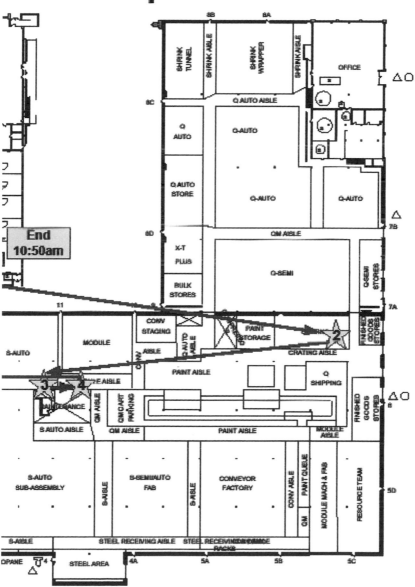

When Bob left, I set up a big whiteboard in my office and translated what he said into plain American English. (Bob's English can be a bit professorial, and he is British.) I invited my top management team in, starting with Gina McIntosh, director of operations, and Steve Clifford, director of manufacturing. Gina had been with Lantech for 35 years and done nearly every job in the building except maybe welding and sales. She arrived at work before dawn most days and was one of the most even-tempered people I had ever met. Steve was the new guy with just 30 years at Lantech. He was a farmer when not running the manufacturing operations, and I was pretty sure he could make a workable jig out of a single nail and a piece of string.[12] These were people who knew how to get things done.

To their credit, they listened with calm interest to the description of how we were going to completely change their working day—even when I outlined the daily standardized work they would be expected to do. I sketched a map of how information would be collected and flow upward to help them do their jobs and they got it.

I will not say that we immediately understood exactly how this thing would work or transform the business. But Gina, Steve, and I saw the good points and trusted Bob enough by that time to know that we should give it a try. On my whiteboard, we laid out a path through the plant and the whole company for our daily gemba walk. We noted where we would stop, whom we would talk to there, and what kind of questions we might ask.

How we approached our team leaders with questions would make a big difference. We wanted to make it clear that we were not going to show up every morning asking for a report or peppering anyone with questions. If team leaders felt like we were

---

12. Jig: a device that holds a part and guides the tool working on it.

putting them on the spot or wasting their time with superfluous executive busywork, this initiative would fail. We needed to make sure we were there to support the work, to be of assistance to people in the next management layer down, to help with problems they could not fix within their functional area.

So we pulled together the two dozen folks who make up Lantech's top two layers of management (*see chart on page 28*). We outlined the problem we were trying to solve and the idea of the daily management system, emphasizing that we needed to structure our gemba walks and meetings in such a way as to be useful to the front line. But we knew we could not show up every morning and say, "What can we do for you today?" We would get blank stares and shrugs. A critical part of the routine, then, would be for the team leaders to collect data that would be relevant to the area and help to bring problems to the surface.

Every department manager—from finance, sales, and IT, to HR, operations, etc.—was asked to find two quality metrics that were easily collectible and had a direct effect on the quality seen by the customer. These would be our metrics to help start conversations at the board that would be deeper than "How are you doing?"

For instance, customer service immediately identified dropped calls—when customers abandoned the call rather than wait for us to pick up—as its most important metric. Engineering decided to track design-change notices, which are generated in operations to alert engineers that an item cannot be built as drawn, and the department's rate of on-time finished drawings. Every work cell in manufacturing opted to use "defects per machine" as one of its metrics. And finance started tracking "days sales outstanding" for receivables. In most cases, this information was already being tracked in various software programs, so we had history on the issue.

Lantech's Top Two Layers of Management

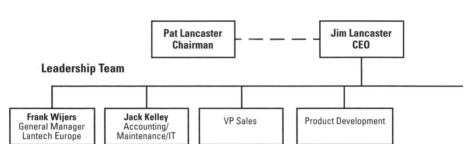

We were not, however, looking for historical problems to fix. We were not looking to re-create crime scenes. Experience has proven to me that people can have a much greater effect on productivity and quality when we fix something that broke five minutes ago rather than last week's issue—no matter how big or thought-provoking. So that's what we aimed for: the metrics that would allow us to see whether performance was deteriorating right now, to know whether the sand castle needed maintenance. All of the old barrier boards came down.

All the folks in that meeting also agreed to go out and build their own management boards. For this, we used 4 x 8-foot sheets of plastic and fiberboard paneling. This is the same material designed for use in inexpensive bathrooms. The panels are big, cheap, and available at almost any home-improvement store, and they act like big dry-erase boards. People could tape plastic sheets to them, creating pockets to store and display their updated data graphs. They could scrawl notes and erase them when issues were resolved. Those big panels might have cost $10 each, and most of our boards were only half of a panel.

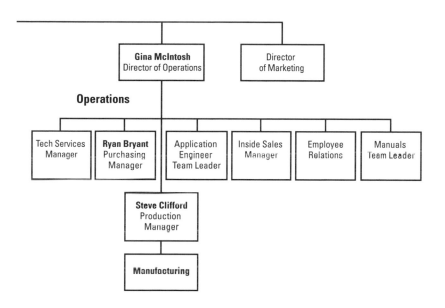

In each area, the boards were screwed to walls or cabinets or cubicles where they could be easily seen, where people would naturally congregate, and as close to everyone's work as possible. There were no boards in break rooms. We decided on a few standards for presenting information on the board. Improvement activities to raise the level of performance always went on the right side of the board, while daily issues about maintaining performance went on the left. But mostly, we wanted those boards to be useful to the people on the front line. These were the boards where the cross-functional management team would meet every morning, but they were not really for our benefit. They were a communication tool for team leaders and production-line leaders, as well as a development opportunity for the team leader.

If I remember right, we gave the managers a week to find their metrics and report back. Some of them required a bit of extra guidance, but mostly, they seemed to get it right away. They collected data on those metrics—almost all of which we had readily available—and calculated the 90-day run rate. If the metric for Q-Semi was defects per machine, for instance, the manager pulled those defects data out of the system for the past 90 days and divided the defects by machines made. That was the run rate.

Then they had another week to put up their boards and start meeting with their own direct reports to ask the standard morning questions: what happened yesterday, and what do you need today? They talked about the run rates for their identified metrics, too, so everyone got used to looking it, asking each other, "So why did we have more defects yesterday than average?" They got a one-week head start on us to get used to the new standardized morning.

We called the morning walks WAR, for *walk-around review*, and we called the boards WAR boards. The first WAR was held in the first working week of 2008. They have continued without interruption, four days a week, ever since.[13] Eight years after we first began this practice, not much has changed in the general outline because it works.

---

13. Operations at Lantech works a four-day week with 10-hour shifts.

Management System Roll Up in Manufacturing

6:00–6:15 a.m.

Work cell team leaders meet with their direct reports, collecting information on the day's schedule, needs, and any foreseeable problems in each production area.

6:15–6:30 a.m.

Production-line team leaders meet with their work cell leaders to review the metrics from the day before to see whether any deterioration has happened and then to support their getting on track. Coaching on problem solving might happen here, and issues that cannot be resolved within that team are carried by the production-line team leaders to the next level of WAR meetings. Who is doing what on which issues is documented on the board so that communication and expectations are clear and visible.

6:30–7:00 a.m.

Production-line team leaders meet with the materials manager, the resources team leader,[14] and the production manager serving all of operations to report on immediate needs and issues.

7:00–8:00 a.m.

The production manager begins the WAR of operations, meeting first with the shipping team leader to collect information on metrics that have deteriorated, barriers for work that day, etc. This continues on to the WAR boards and team leaders of each product line and area within manufacturing—such as assembly, paint, conveyors, electrical, welding, etc.—to get that same information.

---

14. The resources team contains a few specialized floaters—such as a welder, a machinist, etc.—and general assembly workers who fill in for absences and help out with spikes in production needs or problem solving. The resources manager also helps identify needs and places people in temporary assignments.

7:00–7:30 a.m.
Meanwhile, the materials team leader is meeting with schedulers and materials handlers to learn about current conditions and issues.

8:00–9:00 a.m.
Technical services, sales operations, engineering, configuration/ documentation, company services, and product development all have frontline meetings between associates and their team leaders. Once again, the agenda is to review run rates on metrics, discuss actions to take, and assess any barriers to successful work today.

9:00–10:30 a.m.
Senior leaders, including the CEO (on Mondays), director of operations, and a rotating cast of senior leaders from through- out the company, do a 90-minute WAR of the entire company, beginning with product development at 9:00 a.m. then moving straight to shipping.[15] The senior-leadership WAR then goes to materials, production, technical services, engineering, procure- ment, sales, marketing, and HR. The manager of each area meets us at their board where we talk about any metrics that are below the run rate and therefore red. We discuss the business challenges of the day and how we might immediately address problems in operations, which is our first priority.

On Fridays, when operations are generally shut down, we do a more extensive WAR in support services, including IT, HR, and finance. I also attend this WAR when I am in town. These meetings often take a little longer than the 5-minute daily stand-up

---

15. Not every senior leader can break free to do the 90-minute walk every day, but all are strongly encouraged to attend at least once a week, and extended absences are noted. Leaders who cannot attend should send a direct report to represent the functional area and facilitate that person's training.

WAR Activity Cascading Upward from Manufacturing

6:00–6:15 am
Team level
Operators
meet with
Team leader

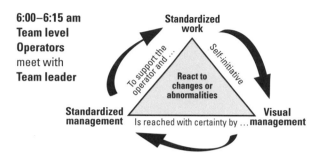

6:15–7:00 am
Cell level
Team leaders
meet with
Factory leader

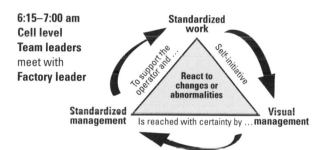

7:00–8:00 am
Production level
Factory leaders
meet with
Manufacturing manager

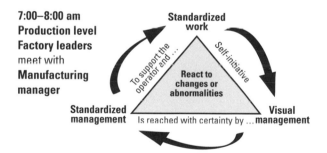

9:00–10:30 am
Department level
Manufacturing manager
meets with
Senior leaders

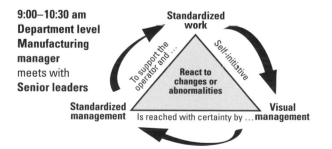

WAR, simply because we have them only once a week and sometimes the issues are more complex. It is a very rare day, however, when the meetings exceed 15 or 20 minutes.

The WAR map is a skeleton of our management system, and every line can be seen as a vital bit of structure. This is what all of our connective tissue hangs on—this daily, scripted, standardized check-in at every critical point in our business. Because these are all people with individual idiosyncrasies, however, it is nothing like robotic. To see what I mean, it will be helpful to tag along in the next chapter as we walk through a morning WAR in Louisville and then in the Netherlands where needs were just a little different.

Chapter 3

Finding the Rhythm of the WAR

D o you remember that excited, clammy-handed feeling on the day you got your very first car? You knew your life was about to change; you just were not sure how.

On the morning of our first walk-around review (WAR) on the first working day of 2008, that's how I felt. I had been told to stay away as people were building their WAR boards and metrics and practicing for the morning review. Now, the moment was finally here to go see how this system would work.

Before setting out, Gina and I had one last check-in about what we were going to do and how. I had two goals for the morning: find out what today's problems might be before they snowballed and make sure people felt supported in their work. I was still a little unsure about that last part. I thought I knew how to support people; I just wasn't used to thinking about how people might feel when I was finished being supportive, if you catch my meaning. And I needed to make sure that everyone knew that I did not necessarily know what to do. I did not have all the answers. For a guy who was used to running a business he had known all his life, it felt a little counterintuitive.

Bob, Gina, and I had talked a lot about coaching versus problem solving. I knew I needed to put a check on my natural instinct to offer up the right answer, but we also needed to know when to pick up the ball.

We created a little test to help guide us. When the problem was most likely contained within the immediate work area or department, we said, we should focus on coaching the manager or team leader on the best way to go about problem solving. If the issue seemed to originate in another area, we would discuss a course of action, and then Gina or I would take ownership of the next steps. We were there not to speculate or hypothesize about a problem's probable source but to coach people to go and look for root causes and then develop plans of attack.

For local problems, we coached. For systemic problems— such as moving associates out of a cell that was down for the day to an area where extra help was needed—we picked up the ball. With cross-functional leadership gathered, many issues can get solved immediately, on the fly.

We started the operations WAR closest to the customer, in shipping at 9:30 a.m. The team leader was working nearby and happy to drop what he was doing and come over to show us his board. It was like that everywhere in the beginning—people in shipping and materials and engineering were all happy to show off their WAR boards and tell us about their data and what they had learned so far. On display in shipping were the run rates for their two quality measures and what those numbers were yesterday. There was also an atomic clock with a note as to what time the WAR was expected to begin and end every morning.

That last item—the atomic clock—was a promise to people in the area that we would be mindful of their time. It was doubly important for me to see those noted times because I have a tendency to become entirely absorbed in what is happening in front of me. Without a clear ending time, I might never make it to the next stop.

In those first weeks, staying on schedule was very difficult. In just about every area, people were already making changes based upon their daily quality tracking, and there was a lot of excitement.

I should explain here that those run rates—showing the actual performance of a process in the past 90 days—were new to us. Bob had been adamant that we track the run rate instead of a quality goal or target. He said improvement happens only when we are looking closely at what is instead of what we hope for.

So at the end of 2007, we had every functional department select two quality metrics, collect their data on those metrics for the previous 90 days, find the daily average—the run rate—and put it up on the left side of the WAR board. Whether the metric was dropped calls in customer service, defects per machine in production, percent on-time in shipping, or overdue invoices in accounting, we wanted to look at how quality performance on a daily basis compared to the previous quarter. So, every day the area leader would post the quality metrics from yesterday beside the corresponding run rate.

When yesterday's numbers fell outside the previously defined run-rate tolerance, the area manager turned a laminated card on the WAR board from green to red, and we would ask, "What was different about yesterday?" The idea here was to find immediate problems—erosions to the sand castle—like processes at the heart of our work and fix them immediately.

The last item on the left side of every WAR board is the quality loop (*see page 38*). This is not at all like the complicated spirals you might find in a business-school workbook. It is a simple what-why-when-who chart on each board to follow progress toward solving each problem.

Example of a Quality Loop

Quality loops have just five lines for five problems because nobody can actively track more than that, we believe. Every time a quality metric went red, we could start a new quality loop entry by stating the problem, listing the next action to be taken, and noting who would report back and when. This form would also be our most important coaching opportunity, as we would always hand a dry-erase maker to the manager or team leader and discuss the issue while coaching the team leader on addressing problems and filling out the form.

It was surprising how quickly things started to change. As soon as people were looking at their quality numbers every day, they began taking action—often before we even had time to coach them. It was like putting up a poster of a thermometer in a fundraising phone bank. People kept an eye on how they were doing, and the sight of it spurred them to more action. So we spent extra time in each area on our walks, talking through specific plans or the results of their investigations—not just talking about a general awareness of a problem. Customer service, for instance, was already working on a system to easily identify how many of the dozen or so phone operators were available to take a call, to ensure that they did not all take lunch breaks or turn off the phone to do paperwork at the same time.

Then we realized that some of the most valuable information we got came as an aside. As we were preparing to walk on from a WAR huddle, I liked to ask, "Is there anything else keeping your area from having a good day?"

It was then that I would often hear about some "little" problem that seemed unfixable, i.e., a certain vendor was always late in filling orders, or another department just didn't seem to understand their needs. I cannot tell you how many times this information solved mysteries or opened doors to discovering a deeper problem. It was incredibly useful, but as a consequence, for the first several months our 90-minute daily senior-leader WAR almost always took at least twice the time allotted.

While I was there at the WAR board, managers started finding other ways for me to be useful. Mostly, they were asking for permissions. A manager might ask whether their group could change their shift's lunch break in order to make the schedule work better. I would ask about the impact on other areas and then most likely say, "Sure," and everyone would be happy. It was convenient to have the CEO's attention and get a quick decision.

Those quick answers had a dark side, though. I discovered that granting permissions is like a gateway drug to micromanaging. Soon, I found myself forgetting my role and making suggestions. If the sales force was having trouble tracking a metric, I knew a good solution for that. After all, I had run the sales department for years. Or I would ask my colleagues on the paint line whether they had considered trying this idea I had. (I felt I was a paint expert too.) If only they looked at the problem from this other angle, they would see the path was obvious.

One time, as we walked away from a WAR board discussion like that, I remember feeling like I had an extra spring in my step. It was fun to walk around fixing things. I felt really useful. That's about when Gina put her hand on my arm and gently asked, "Do you really think that was the kind of help they needed?"

I had fallen into the exact trap that Gina and I had tried to guard against. She reminded me of our first job out there: coaching the managers to investigate problems with their teams. We needed to teach them to see problems and then to address them using lean thinking. If they did not begin doing this on their own, I might as well be paint line leader for life.

The problem was I had worked in just about every area of Lantech and I really thought I knew what was going on. Give me any set of facts and I could offer a solution or a line of inquiry right quick. I once thought it was my greatest strength; now I have learned that it's a great shortcoming. I have talked to many leaders of other organizations who have told me they have a similar problem or the same problem in reverse. Some leaders feel an inadequate depth of knowledge about certain operations and try to mask their unease with little lectures on what they do know. Pontificating on what you know and spitting out quick answers are perfectly natural consequences of the way most of us think about being a boss, but they are not very helpful.

On the manufacturing floor, people are used to this sort of behavior from bosses. They appear to accept it, but as soon as my back was turned, they were probably rolling their eyes at yet another "helpful suggestion" from a suit. The offices were a different story.

The people there are used to being given a task and then getting the space to do the work as they see fit. They're professionals with independent knowledge of their fields, and it was very clear that I was infringing on their territory. As I got more confident on our review walks, people in the offices were becoming more defensive.

If Gina had not pulled me up short, we might have had real trouble on our hands. Soon, managers probably would have started feeding me information to keep me happy instead of information that was actually useful. Gina had been worried about the same thing. She had this little card taped to the clipboard she carried on our WAR rounds, reminding her about how questions needed to be asked. The card had bullet points like, "Ask questions. Don't make statements. Watch your tone. Check body language."

Gina mostly worried about pulling a grimace in the face of bad news, like a red card displayed on a WAR board, indicating that the group was not meeting schedule or had quality metrics falling below the run rate. I had to train myself to feel excitement when I saw a red card and to think, "There's an opportunity," instead of, "Oh no, a problem."

A lot of people have to work hard at this. It took some of our managers years to stop being defensive in the face of a red card, to stop rushing to explain away the underlying facts. And every time we elevate someone into the position of manager, we need to give special training until they see the color red as an opportunity instead of an indictment.

As we continued with our WAR, it took real discipline to remember that we were not standing at the boards to solve problems. We were standing there to ensure that the business of problem solving was happening as it should. If the problem transcended a functional area, that's when we stepped in to help with actual problem solving.

For example, if the folks in accounting were trying to solve an issue related to late billing, my job was to talk them through the elements of PDCA problem solving. If they were having an issue with billing because they were not getting on-time bill of materials (BOM) on custom jobs from engineering, Gina and I would decide which one of us would follow up with engineering later in the day. Of course, engineering would immediately pick up the issue if the engineering manager was on the WAR.

I have heard from leaders of similar initiatives in other organizations that, compared to others, we began this process with baby steps. Other organizations have begun a daily management review with a full scorecard of quality, safety, delivery, and cost measures on their huddle boards—what we call WAR boards—in functional areas. And it's true that in Louisville we now track a half dozen or so metrics at each area, in alignment with company-wide strategy.

Our careful start with just two quality metrics was the right approach for Lantech because we needed to get the right habits in place. In fact, I think that a successful daily management walk around should always spring from the needs and temperament of the frontline touch labor and their managers, not from the CEO's needs or corporate needs or some theoretical template.

To see what I mean, let's look at Lantech's European operation. This is a plant that makes case-erector machines in a picturesque town called Cuijk in the eastern Netherlands. Cuijk (pronounced "cow-k") is actually a prehistoric town; its existence is recorded on the oldest road map of the Roman Empire. And I think the leadership team in 2008 would agree that many of their habits were nearly as entrenched as ancient wheel ruts.

This case-erector company had begun its life as Rembrandt Packaging. They made good machines that I first saw at a trade show in France. Immediately, I wanted to add their machines to our suite of products. It took me three years to convince the owner/founder to sell the company to me.

I knew going in that all those good machines were built with a handcrafted approach, with lots of tinkering and adjustment, instead of the lean system we used at Lantech. In 2002 they had neither real work standardization nor a tight plan for how material flowed through the plant. So we did a lot of training on lean ideas and put in a one-piece-flow production line. Once lean thinking began to take hold, we ramped up production without adding people and became much more reliable at predicting output and quality. We could then sell a lot more case erectors through our US distribution channels.

Those first few years after the sale were also taken up with cosmetic integration. we became each other's distributors, we found ways to enter markets together as a unified end-of-production-line solution; we redesigned their machines to be a uniform Lantech blue.

By 2007, they were stable and producing machines at a reliable rate. Sales had grown, and they were hiring more people, building up from their tiny base of 35 very close-knit employees. But they were not making much money. I replaced their lean-resistant general manager with a transplant from Louisville to start the process first and then found a young Dutch engineer named Frank Wijers (pronounced "wires"), who was energetic and eager to learn new methods. Their margins improved a little but not enough to ride out any significant setbacks.

On a planning visit, I sat down with top management and explained to them that they were running the business like a hobby—like an activity that they all found fascinating, but as if it had little to do with money. Hobbies cost money, I explained. Businesses make money, and they needed to start making some. Every pair of eyes turned in my direction showed that they were offended. But after that, things changed.

"At the time, we all felt like we were working like crazy, but we couldn't seem to make money," Frank remembers. "There was a lot of rework all the time. We did so much nonvalue-added work that we couldn't see it. If someone had to walk for a tool, that's just the way it was. You walk to get a tool and have a little chat about soccer on the way. We always had a list of issues to fix on a machine before it shipped. It was normal."

As reality set in, I heard that people feared the company—and their jobs—would move to Poland without them. Labor is cheaper there, and it is fewer than 500 miles away. So, I told them I would help them find higher margins if they would change their way of working and sent Bob Morgan to Cuijk to help out. It would be up to them whether they listened.

Frank and his team began with reorganizing the work. They created better work flows that did not involve searching for tools or parts. Focusing first on their most popular case-erector machine as a model cell, they set about making the work more visual, so people could see what was happening, and standardized it. That activity made Frank realize some troubling things about the way he and his management team worked, too.

"All of us were juggling ten thousand things, and our days were full of meetings and e-mail. But we had no idea, really, if we were working on the same things or even talking about the same things," Frank says. "We did not have any visuals."

Realizing this, the team in Cuijk started doing WAR rounds earlier in their transformation process than we did in Louisville. They began in the case-erector assembly area but quickly added in the other functional areas. It was not a large plant at this point, probably 60 employees in all. And because they all needed to be on the same page, the entire management team went together on the whole walk-around review every morning. All 10 managers—who had worked and socialized together for years—went together to every stop and argued all the way.

"This WAR opened our eyes," Frank says. "We thought we knew, but we did not."

From four stops in assembly and subassembly, to shipping, the production board, inside sales, and then sales and marketing, the entire Dutch team would stop and listen to what was happening that day, and then everyone would start talking at once.

The way Frank describes it sounds like a rolling, slightly comical rugby scrum. It was messy and loud and probably necessary for them in Cuijk. After years of managing through e-mail and spreadsheets, always at some remove from the work, managers needed to agree on what they were looking at. They needed to find common understanding. And the managers desperately needed to get closer to the problem of the day, to understand in a granular way how the work got done.

For instance, an important moment in the life of every machine they built was its first test. They almost always did a final test with the customer present—sometimes by live video feed—but the first test was the most important. Standard operating procedure in the old days was for the first test to produce a punch list of items to be fixed or modified. Rework was so common that nobody thought of it as waste.

Once they started measuring defects per machine and then began investigating the causes of those defects, they began realizing how interconnected the whole operation was. Machine defects were not just the responsibility of production anymore.

"What we really needed to see, I think, were the struggles that were going on in each department and especially in production. When we traced back how the struggles in operations started, we kept seeing that it started in sales or engineering or procurement, but in the end, it was the operators on the front line who were solving it," Frank says. "They were doing all of this corrective work. It took a lot of time, and none of us in the other areas really knew that we were starting these problems."

It may have been necessary, but thankfully, the rolling scrum did not last long. As the arguing died down and agreements were made, team members started making sense of who should attend what part of the walk-around review and how to ensure that all necessary information flowed up while support for the work flowed down.

Eventually, you could stand in one spot and see 75% of the walk-around review in Cuijk. It began each morning with team leaders in the four production areas gathering information and talking about the day's work with their teams. As work began, each team leader moved to their production board to meet with the production support WAR, including engineers, a materials leader, and the production leader, Theo Voss.

Then within sight of every production area, Theo met with leaders from logistics and procurement, controls engineering, and mechanical engineering at his production WAR board to discuss specific frontline needs. Frank joined this group to listen for the day's issues and help find solutions.

This group then walked over to shipping. Shipping was added to the daily walk-around review much later, in 2015, after they saw the shipping manager chasing each individual machine to see whether it was really ready. Of every machine, the manager was asking whether the final test had been arranged with the customer, either in person or by video, whether shipping methods had been approved, and international regulations satisfied. Once Frank and his team realized that the shipping manager was the only one who knew what was arranged and what was not, they worked quickly to make that information visual.

From there, Frank met with the inside-sales team to discuss build quotes. The inside-sales team prepares quotes for both standard and custom machines. They translate customer needs into engineering and manufacturing orders so machines can be built. The outside-sales team visits customers and helps them decide on the right solutions and negotiate commercial terms.

Here, we ask whether we are meeting customer expectations for quote turnaround times and other such quality metrics for this department. They have run rates for their quality metrics and andon cards indicating a red or green status. We also look at the content of the ordering queue and the rolling build schedule, which is populated as orders come in.

After this meeting, managers from engineering, accounting, service, and procurement arrive for the inside-sales support team meeting. Like every stand-up meeting in front of a board, these last 10–15 minutes and provide the kind of information people need to guide their energies for the rest of the day.

By the end of 2008, the team in Cuijk began to get into a rhythm. They were uncovering problems they never expected, tracing those issues back to the source, and taking corrective action. What really surprised Frank, though, was how much easier his day became. He was finding problems, helping to guide people toward solutions, and he no longer felt as though he was juggling like mad. He and his team listened to Bob like we did in Louisville but proceeded in a different way because they had a different reality—and yet still arrived at the same place we did in Louisville. We all had a lot less chaos and a little more breathing room.

All of this happened just in time. By early 2008, I knew that some very serious economic storm clouds were gathering. I became more cautious in hiring and stretched out other decisions while waiting to see whether the bad signs in the United States would blow over. Then in August of that year, orders coming in suddenly dropped in half. We had seen slowdowns before, but the velocity of this drop nearly gave me a nosebleed. While news of the mortgage default crisis was sweeping the country and members of Congress were arguing about who was too big to fail, I started getting ready for our biggest annual trade show in Chicago.

I had a lot to worry about. Mostly, businesses buy our equipment when they are putting in new production lines and expanding capacity. Someday our customers may buy capital equipment to replace old machines, but ours is still a fairly young company in a young industry, and we build durable machines. So we are only starting to see replacement business. We rely for the great bulk of our sales on expansion, and this requires optimism. To invest in new equipment, our customers need to see an uptick in business and to believe that more upticks are likely. When sales drop even 2%, business people get cautious. A small swing in the GDP makes for tsunamis in the capital equipment sector.

I knew all of this as I arrived at that trade show with four tractor-trailer loads of beautiful new machines, all shiny and polished and ready to sell. I put on my best suit and stood in my 7,000-square-foot show booth, and as the first day kicked off, I heard the distinct sound of crickets out there in the hall. This normally bustling trade show was like a ghost town, and we would need to scramble to survive.

Considering the orders we already had in the pipeline, we had about 90 days at best before business dried up. At 50% of sales, we could not break even. So, I decided to resize the company for breakeven at 50% of current business, a challenge much worse than what I had faced in 2001 when the drop was only 14%. This required a heartbreaking 10% layoff. A more aggressive manager might have cut deeper, but I had other plans.

Once we recalculated takt time for half of the customer demand rate and freed up a lot of associates from their work areas, we redeployed our best people to work on cost savings or on design improvements to our machines. In years past, this might have meant putting these people in the Kaizen Promotion Office to lead improvement-team efforts. But this time, I put some people in the new-product department to work on improvements and left the rest of them in their functional areas with a new full-time job assignment: attack costs.[16]

At this point, cost metrics joined quality metrics on the WAR boards, and every day we asked where we were wasting money. I started personally signing all of the outgoing checks to find opportunities.

Soon, the ideas for where to save money were coming in thick and fast. Instead of buying disposable wet wipes to degrease our hands, we could use towels and a laundry service. Instead of renting trash dumpsters, we would buy them. (I had no idea we were paying for those unsightly dumpsters every month until I started writing the checks.) We emptied the contents of rented storage containers into the building and sent the containers away. We found many parts that were less expensive to make in-house with our extra capacity.

A lot of companies encourage suggestions. The difference at Lantech was that, instead of putting out a passive box with a slot for idea cards, top management was showing up every morning in

---

16. This was the end of the KPO as we had known it because we discovered that line managers with good problem-solving skills could lead their teams to find and address problems without the need for staff experts. We may re-create the KPO in future, however, as it is a good place to train up-and-coming managers in continuous-improvement skills necessary for their line assignments.

the work areas, listening to everyone's ideas for improvement and cost savings, and then making decisions on the spot. People saw their ideas approved and supported quickly and were encouraged to come up with more.

By this point, everyone knew the whole country was in trouble. The nightly news was filled with stories of companies shutting down, homes and jobs lost. When disaster strikes, we all want to help out—to join a bucket line or give blood or anything that might be of assistance.

What we did at Lantech was simply give our people an outlet for that impulse. Using the daily management system, I was touching 350 people each day, in person or by proxy, with the same message: let's save our company by cutting costs. It was a powerful force.

As the year moved on, we got better at the WARs. They became more brief and precise, even as the new cost metrics were added on everyone's boards. We kept knocking out the money-savings idea, and as the Great Recession went global and began rolling across Europe, Frank Wijers added cost metrics to his boards and also began urgently soliciting money-saving ideas. In Cuijk, they unscrewed half of the light bulbs in the offices, canceled all the magazine subscriptions, stopped scheduling overtime, and most importantly, worked feverishly to remove material costs from the equipment through multiple iterations of cost-saving design improvements.

Each action we took, viewed independently, might seem too insignificant to matter. It might seem as if we were counting paper clips while a lot of people were arguing for launching the life rafts. Yet, all of those hundreds or even thousands of little actions added up to some astounding results.

At the end of that very bad year, our gross margin had improved by 7 points. Material costs dropped from 39% of sales to 32%. That meant, after the cost of materials and direct labor, we were netting 25% more cash on every machine we sold. We never fell below the breakeven point.

Instead, 2009 was a nicely profitable year, and we were in position to make the years even better moving ahead. The gift that the Great Recession left us, as you will see in the next chapter, was in forcing us to change the outmoded way we had thought about the work of management.

Chapter 4

Information Flows Up;
Support Flows Down

N othing focuses the mind like constraint. Even though we were making more money per machine than we had in 2007, orders were still not bouncing back.

Not even close. As 2009 became 2010, I kept doing the walk-around review every day. I had planned to cut back to once a week, but being close to the work kept providing such big benefits that I did not want to stop.

This meant I was walking the same path, talking to the same people, asking the same questions for 90 or 120 minutes every morning. If I ever thought that being a CEO would be glamorous, these years certainly disabused me of that notion.

When you keep to the same routine every morning, I found, you have a choice. You can sleepwalk through it, or you can look for fresh details to keep your interest. I kept interested by noticing how people reacted to Gina and me and to each other and how energy rose and fell depending on how we phrased questions and requests. Before this time, I might have said that management was my expertise. But now, I was learning what being a manager actually meant. This day-in, day-out routine that looks really dull on paper started to become fascinating.

Learning to pay close attention to how others reacted to me and how they *received* my management was even more important than I knew at the time. This daily management system turns some expectations upside down. It is set up so that information flows up while support flows down. For the system to work, everyone must agree that we all work for the front line instead of for the front office. It is a radical departure from most people's expectations about work.

For instance, let's say that your boss and your subordinate walk into your office at the exact same moment, talking. You can catch only a word here or there, but your boss is talking about something their boss needs for a board meeting, while your subordinate is talking about a sudden problem with a customer order. Every fiber of our self-interested beings has been tuned to tell the subordinate to wait while we turn our full attention to the boss. This, I learned, is exactly the wrong response.

When we favor the needs of the people who are actually creating value, we are favoring the continued ability of the company to create revenue. The boss is rarely the person creating value. Remember that value is determined by what the customer will pay for. In my experience, customers are willing to pay for real goods and services, not graphs and presentation slides and other tools of management.

That makes sense, right? So why do most people firmly believe that we should act in the opposite way? Partly because we want to seem useful to our boss, and therefore, employed. But there is also business-school reasoning here, rooted in a superficial understanding of productivity that we might call the "False Value of the Most Expensive."

Decades ago, creators of the Toyota Production System warned against this when they saw factory managers running the most expensive machines as much as possible on the theory that the more parts a machine created, the more its initial cost was offset or justified. In reality, this caused overproduction of some parts and needless inventory. In health care, this same fallacy has caused people to arrange the work to accommodate the needs of one highly paid surgeon instead of the combined needs (and costs) of the team of doctors, nurses, and technical specialists creating value for the patient.

In every industry, people make the mistake of thinking that we should support the productivity of the boss, making a six-figure salary, over the productivity of a $30,000-a-year machine operator or welder or transactions clerk. If we save the boss 30 minutes worth of work, the thinking goes, we will have created more value than if we saved an operator's 30 minutes of work.

This kind of thinking is a trap, especially in the case of six-figure bosses who do not create revenue. Let me be clear: managers and executives are useful to the extent they can make direct-value creators more efficient and effective. Yet very little of their time is spent actually doing this. So, bosses are not a resource that we should optimize. In general, bosses bring value to the business only when they improve the work of the people creating value.

Anyway, in my experience, we never make more money by optimizing a single machine or person. We make more money only when the entire ecosystem produces more with less. Because boss favoring is such an ingrained reaction, we need to guard against this tendency at every turn.

On a daily basis, this simple equation has helped us focus:

revenue producing = immediate attention

Still, I had to train subordinates to put me and my needs behind the needs of the front line, which is exactly as hard as it sounds. Only if my needs were directly related to value production should I be considered of equal importance. And every time a new manager comes on board, we need to teach the lesson and break the habits all over again. People often have funny ideas of how a person in charge should behave. Even if the new manager comes from within Lantech, rising to a management position almost always requires extensive coaching on how to prioritize incoming issues.

This requires close listening and clarity of purpose. For instance, I try to make it clear that we support the front line first because it makes sense to do so. This is not an experiment in socialism. This is not to prove our love and respect for the hourly wage earner. We support the front line first simply because those are the people creating whatever the customer wants to buy— whether a physical object or a service such as technical support. The front line creates revenue and, therefore, value. If we focus first on value creation, we make money. And making money is how a business stays open.

This simplified view of the business environment has led to some significant money savings. As we did our daily walk-around reviews, we were always reminding ourselves and each other of our purpose: support efforts to create value. As I wrote checks to pay bills, I did the same simplification: if the money was not being spent to create well-made products that allow our customers to ship goods without damage, it was waste.

That was how I found myself questioning one of the hallmarks of lean thinking: *just-in-time* delivery. Or really, that was how I found an expensive example of faux lean thinking that had been allowed to continue for a decade.

In the late 1990s and continuing into the new century, Lantech employees were told that inventory is waste and that we needed our upstream partners to deliver what we needed exactly when we needed it. Contracts were set up with vendors to ensure that we would receive their goods in small amounts frequently. But the suppliers were never producing to order in one-piece flow in immediate response to our orders.

For example, metal fabricators that supplied us with parts were making them in 30- or 90-day batches and storing all these parts on shelves to be delivered as we needed. They were paying for that inventory, which meant we were ultimately paying for the inventory in the price per piece.

In one case, our upstream partner was actually buying motors in bulk at a significant discount (to him), storing them in a warehouse in Indianapolis, and then using a dedicated employee to ship us the motors just-in-time. So there was an extra person in the value chain and lots of storage and handling, which was reflected in the higher per-piece part price we were being charged. We had only pushed the waste upstream and were spending 15% more to maintain the fiction.

In short order, we bought a couple of truckloads of those motors, found a convenient spot for racks to store them, and started collecting the discount ourselves. The waste of big-batch production was still in the system, of course, but at least we were not paying extra per piece just to keep waste hidden upstream. A company our size can influence some supply chains and not others.

Seeing the waste of that inventory on our own shelves every day means we are constantly reminded of the need to reduce it somehow. And the incident gave me the opportunity to explain to our procurement team that our most important goal was not inventory reduction. It is good if the trade-off makes sense. But our real goal was to sell and support machines that could secure our customers' loads for safe shipment. That meant making good-quality machines, cost effectively.

Procurement's job was to make sure all materials arrived at the front line when needed at the lowest total cost. Creating a lean value chain, end to end, is a great goal because there is a huge amount of waste to be attacked.

A lean value chain is not, however, as simple as just-in-time deliveries to our facility. The wrong message had been allowed to persist in procurement because I was too far away from the work to know it was happening. The people doing the work in procurement thought our purchasing practices were dumb, but they figured there was some cost-of-money argument, some financial mumbo jumbo that balanced it all out.

What I learned is that when I write the checks, just as when I am setting strategy, I need to be down in the work on a regular basis to see the outcomes—the received messages—of my decisions. Instead of just sending a message, I have realized, I need to loop back and look at how my message is heard and acted upon.

In fact, being in the work on a regular basis changed everything about the way I manage people. When I was on the paint line, we were making decisions based on tangible facts. If you held the spray gun one way or another, you could see the results and make decisions accordingly. On the daily walk-around review, we would see a metric in red ink, ask a few questions, and then be able to speak directly to the operator who saw an error and stopped the work. I found great comfort in immediate and concrete information.

Before the daily management system, I would often find myself fidgeting through long meetings with executives who had very nice-looking presentations and graphs. We would all sit together in the boardroom—the highest-paid people in my company—and argue heatedly about things that needed to be done, many of which were probably not going to happen anyway.

Once a week, each one of my direct reports would also appear in my office for one-on-one meetings. We would discuss key performance indicators and talk about objectives for the quarter or the year. My top managers filled me in on the environment in their departments, the reactions of their people, and the results of investigations or experiments. The majority of judgments I made were based upon what they told me.

Most of what I saw in their sector of the business was filtered through their view. They would gather up their KPIs and measures, walk to my office, and tell me what they thought I needed to hear. I do not want to make it sound like they were manipulating and hedging. They were editing. They were picking and choosing the details they thought I needed to hear.

From these naturally incomplete reports, I was expected to participate in decision making and judge the executives' performance. It was like managing from a very long distance over a distorted telephone line. Most people do it this way. It is both normal and absurd.

So, it was a revelation to go every morning to operations, sales, marketing, accounting, and product development to see my direct reports in action. In stand-up meetings before WAR boards, we could see what they were working on that day and witness how they managed activities and people.

People behave differently when they are speaking to their direct reports as opposed to their bosses. I suppose this is obvious. But most bosses think we know our subordinates and therefore have a good idea of how they will manage their own subordinates. This is just not true. When the work of management began happening at a specific time and place every day, we could actually see it happening.

And being present for the daily acts of leadership meant that if we had any concerns or questions, we could loop back around after lunch and have a quick chat about what the manager was doing and how. After all, the best way to coach is to stand on the field and watch how everyone plays. If you have only the final score to guide your management attempts, you will not be an effective coach.

I would like to say that my direct reports always appreciated my consistent, daily attention. But anyone who has worked in a company with a few strong personalities will know better. There were times in the beginning when we would consistently hit a wall in one area or another. We senior leaders came to think of it as a big green wall. All performance indicators would be showing green, and we would be assured, "We're good. Everything's great." Meanwhile, the unsaid message was "Move along, move along. We don't need your help."

There were times when I thought of the thousand other things I could have been doing at that moment and was sorely tempted to walk away. If I had, though, I would have been shirking my standardized work and consequently undermining the entire management system.

This management system, after all, is constructed with interlocking pieces of standardized work at each level of the company. In order to support my direct reports, I need to know the content of their standardized work. If I don't know it, I can't coach it. So, let's take a closer look at how we construct standardized work. It's a little different from what we were originally taught during the first phase of our lean transformation in the early 1990s.

Ugly Wallpaper

Anyone who has been inside a company that practices lean thinking has probably seen standardized work in its classic format. In the 1990s, we were taught to define the work steps, sequence them, attach cycle times to the steps, and make it visible. So we did that.

Everywhere, we hung oversized standardized work sheets that had curved icons for people, squares for workstations, arrows showing direction of the work flow, and lists of process steps and cycle times. The more artistic versions might have sketches of hands and tools. Managers at lots of companies point to these illustrations and proudly say, "We have standardized work."

There was a time when we believed this was enough. Like much of our lean effort, however, our understanding of standardized work has evolved over time. Our early understanding was a combination of sketched pictures and words on a form. The words were in English, and the work sequence and cycle times for each step were almost always decided upon and written by an engineer from outside the work area or during a kaizen workshop. These were printed out on big sheets of paper and hung up around a workstation or cell, where before long they were ignored like so much ugly wallpaper.

The presumption was that if the operator just had a clear set of steps and a time frame, they would do the work in that manner and sequence. The truth is operators do their work in the way that is the easiest, least tedious, and most intuitive given the real conditions of the raw material, the tools, and their individual skill level. If that happens to line up with the written standard, then all is well. But when the materials, tools, and skills are not what the frontline associate thinks they should be, it is most likely that the standardized way is not the most intuitive way for the work to be done. So, the real work migrates from the standard.

We knew that standardized work was necessary in a lean environment. Without standards and a stable process, there could be no improvement. It all made so much logical sense that we kept at it instead of admitting the truth.

Finally, with Bob's guidance, we started digging into the big questions. Why were the standardized work sheets ignored? We asked our frontline associates this question, watched their work, and found two answers.

First, there was the issue of respect. If an outside group or engineer came into the cell and announced a new work sequence, a lot of associates would nod and try the new way but revert to their old habits as soon as the outsider left. The common refrain is that outsiders do not really understand the work, pressures, materials, and tools and so fail to see that the operators knew how to do the work the best way in the first place.

Second, anyone who is performing the same task repeatedly knows the work inside of three days and stops looking at the standardized work sheet. It becomes superfluous. Meanwhile, something always changes in the process. We might have a dozen engineering change notices come through every week. Changes to parts, tools, and processes also happen all the time. Yet, rarely was the wallpaper changed to reflect that. So, even if everyone adopted an outside engineer's work sequences, there was a good chance that a number of changes—big and small—caused the standardized work sheets to fall out-of-date quickly, and again, they were ignored.

We needed to graduate past the paper idea of standard work to *standardized work* that includes the human dimension, where the best way to do the work is actually written into the environment. Bob likes to use the analogy of textbooks and poetry.

Let's say you need to memorize 50 lines of text. In the old way—the textbook way—memorization is very hard work and, for many of us, nearly impossible. However, add some rhythm and rhyme, make it poetic and user friendly, and that old text—that still spells out the best way to perform a job—burrows deep into our memories. Creating memorable rhymes is more difficult and time-consuming. But spending the time up front to think about how instructions will be received and remembered by those actually doing the work pays off in the long run.

To create standardized work now, we study a process with the work team, take out the hard and tedious stuff (like memorization), improve upon it by making it easier for people doing the task, and then restructure the work environment so that the new work sequence is as intuitive as possible. When a task is completed, a person's hand should naturally fall upon the tools and materials for the next bit of work. This is intuitive standardized work.

It is not unlike good software. The user interface programs that we call *intuitive* do not require training because each step tends to spring naturally toward the next. Software designers think of the needs of the user at a particular moment in the work sequence and provide for those needs with buttons and cues in places where the eye would naturally fall. Making standardized work requires the same approach: creating an environment where work is facilitated as the associate is led through a sequence of steps in order to create a desired result. The correct way to do the work should always be the easiest and most intuitive way.

Sustainable standardized work should also be flexible enough to adapt to whatever variables get thrown into the mix today. If there are fewer people doing the work, or if the takt time is shorter or longer, a team leader should be able to make a few adjustments in the environment to accommodate the new work needs. If there are parts shortages or quality issues, the work will also throw off signals to a team leader who can then make the appropriate corrections and adjustments.

In the office, it can be software that throws off the signals of a problem or maybe a buildup of files on a desk. In the shop, time is usually the biggest cue. Team leaders can tell at a glance whether material is showing up at the right time or whether one person on a team suddenly has more work to complete than others.[17]

This is why we use a stopwatch to time work steps. We do not want to put operators on the spot or push them to go faster. We simply want to know what is usual when we design work flows so that when it becomes unusual, it is obvious and a team leader or manager can step up with support.

This description of standardized work may make it sound as though it is only for the people on the front line. This is not true. Without some kind of standardized work extending through every layer of management, we could not hope to sustain our daily management system.

Simply put, managers need standardized work in order to be consistently useful to each other and to their direct reports. In the days before our morning walk-around review, we could spend

---

17. This line-of-sight alert system is only possible, of course, because we do not have inventory built up in or between workstations. The just-in-time delivery of materials to the line, implemented in the 1990s, is still in place today and makes much of our visual management system possible.

hours each week trying to track down one person or another and then spring questions on them—questions often requiring some depth of background knowledge—in the parking lot or outside the restroom. Or we would write long e-mails and hope for an answer this week. This is no longer necessary. We know where managers will be every morning, and we come armed with information relevant to both the day's work and ongoing initiatives.

Every manager at Lantech practices standardized work to some degree. When I do my Monday WAR of all areas and departments at Lantech and my Friday morning WAR with the smaller functional areas, I follow the same path each time, trying mightily to stick to the time schedule so that each department head knows when to meet me.

On Tuesday afternoons from 2–4 p.m., I also visit half of Lantech's WAR boards (*see an example of a WAR board on page 66*) to look at the right side in order to assess and support improvement plans. The following week, I review the other half of the Lantech boards. The right half of every WAR board is focused on improvement and shows details of bigger improvement projects that can't be done in a day or even a few days. Along with Gina, our purchasing manager Ryan Bryant, and other leaders who join on a rotating basis, we spend 15 minutes at each area's boards, looking at the A3s used to analyze and solve substantial problems or implement improvements. We search for barriers we can knock down or other ways to support the work and improve the speed of implementation of improvement initiatives.

On Wednesdays at 8:30 a.m., I join Jack Kelley, who manages the company services group, which includes IT, accounting, and maintenance, for a WAR of his disparate departments. The time I spend with Jack includes sand castle maintenance, mentoring, and looking for ways to support this manager who took on so many departments.

Example of a WAR Board

The left side of a WAR board addresses daily issues about maintaining performance. Displays include performance metrics and a quality loop. For example, metrics for the Q-Semi include defects per machine, the run rate, safety, and training.

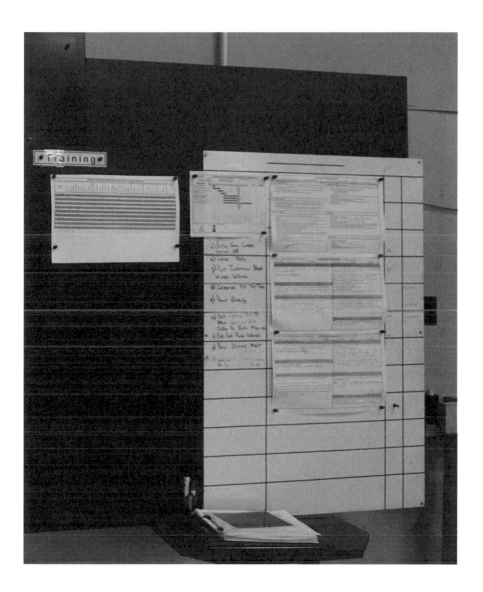

The right side of every WAR board focuses on improvement and shows details of bigger improvement projects that can't be done in a few days. Displays include A3s, business issues, potential countermeasures, and actions.

Also on Wednesday mornings, I have a weekly phone call with Frank Wijers in the Netherlands with a standard agenda, in which we try to virtually walk through the plant together. That adds up to about five hours a week of standardized work for me. My direct reports may have more or less standardized work depending on needs. Gina McIntosh and Frank Wijers have daily walk-around reviews and are responsible for more functional areas and so have more than 10 hours of standardized work each week.

Darryl Gee in sales and Paul Stewart in marketing, which are smaller, more contained departments, need considerably less time to perform their standardized work. They have about an hour each day in which they collect information, provide support to their associates, and conduct their daily WAR report. We also have a quarterly improvement review that involves the top managers in the company and has its own consistent standardized work.

Taking a step closer to the front line we find Karen Froman, a 32-year veteran of Lantech who is the materials manager. In the management hierarchy, Karen is right in the middle and known for her combination of hustle and calm. Her day begins at 6:20 a.m. with the production-line leaders meeting. That's a standard bit of her morning, but her major standardized work begins with her 7 a.m. WAR, from the front of the plant to the back, meeting with all the material handlers to see that they are set up for success that day. That might take an hour. Karen takes another hour to deal with any issues she has found and update her WAR board for the 9 a.m. leadership WAR. She writes down any problems, daily attendance, and parts shortages. She notes the cycle times of her material handlers' daily inventory audit—part of a long-term quality initiative to improve the accuracy of inventory. And she updates the quality loop sheet, which notes how issues are being addressed, along with by whom and when, in her area.

Because Karen has developed an expertise in problem solving and our daily management system, she spends a lot of afternoons helping others around the plant. One team leader might need help understanding why his system for parts replenishment keeps ending in a snarl; another might want help following standardized work on a quality loop issue.

So, Karen might have three hours of standardized work in a day. If standardized work flowed perfectly down the hierarchy, ballooning as it approached the front line, you would expect Karen's direct reports to have 50%–60% of their time devoted to standardized work. However, the seven material handlers who report to Karen have no formal standardized work. They know their jobs and perform them quite well, but we have not done the time and motion studies on materials handling to develop cycle times for every step simply because there has not yet been an urgent need for it.

This is another sign of our recently inverted priorities. It used to be that when we talked about improvement and change, we would turn first to the front line. We would study the work of clerks, welders, and assemblers and make changes to their routines based on the best theories we knew. But in the past few years we have realized that we often need to change the work of leaders first—whether that is a frontline manager or an executive—before we foist new methods onto our value creators.

When we create new standardized work, we rely on one of two methods: workshops and the results of problem solving. Workshops are the environment in which we teach people the purpose of standardized work and how to create it. Held a few times a year, these workshops are taught by one of our employees and are considered part of their education. After an introduction to the improvement ideas, workshop attendees go into a work area as a team and observe several repetitions of the job being performed. There is always variation. We select the best current methods we see for doing the work and then look for ways to improve upon it.

Attendees are taught to watch for any possible safety issues, for people walking around looking for items, and for people having to think about their next step. If someone's face is scrunched up in concentration, that's a good sign that the work is hard and tedious instead of intuitive and simple.

Team members' first job is always to attack safety issues. To remove the hard and tedious work, they document the work steps and time them. They search out the steps that have the most fluctuation in cycle time and focus on improving and stabilizing those.

We try to make the work visible so that the team leader can manage it and observe the standardized work a few more times to make sure it holds up under daily repetition. This is a more time-consuming and challenging way to create standardized work because teams of people need to be brought together and regular work is interrupted back at associates home department, but there is a real advantage in teaching many people how to do this.

The second step in creating standardized work is to chase down a problem, solve it, and create new or revised standardized work to lock in the solution. *(See image at right.)*

A good example of this happened with our procurement department in 2015. Procurement is a four-person team that reports to Ryan Bryant. It's a stable team of seasoned buyers—the kind of team that people might believe does not need standardized work because they know what they are doing. But on the day that a bunch of steel tubes piled up outside of the conveyor shop and a big, expensive machine was suddenly stalled in assembly, I think that Ryan was quite surprised when the problem was traced back to procurement.

Standardized Work for Problem Solving

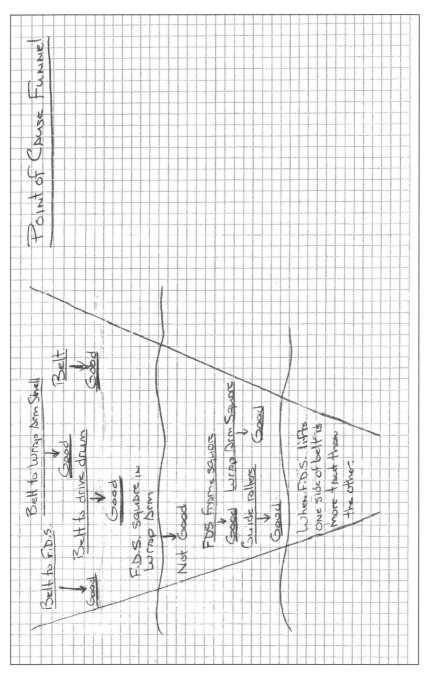

The issue was zinc. Every machine that we ship to Europe needs to have the steel tubes that make up the conveyor bed dipped in zinc to prevent rusting on the trans-Atlantic voyage. Zinc coating is an option that a sales associate writes into an order. It is then a buyer's job to note the option and schedule the truck to take the cut tubes from the conveyor shop to our zinc-plating contractor and back again. One day this didn't happen, and production got snarled. We took a representative from each team that touched the work—purchasing, receiving, sales, engineering, and the conveyor shop—and investigated what happened.

In a rapid-reaction team like this, the job is to pinpoint where the process went from good to bad. As with many multidepartmental processes, communication was the issue. After sales noted the zinc option, there was no trigger to have the buyer order the truck to take the rollers to the plating company. The buyers just knew to do it. Until someone forgot.

All we needed to do was add a line in the electronic scheduling form that prompted the buyer to perform the extra work involved. Then, Ryan and his team wrote out the six steps required for dealing with a zinc-roller option. It was just one of the many details of our process that had never been standardized. Now, anyone who works in procurement can be quickly trained on the process. Since the line was added to the electronic scheduling form, buyers naturally came across the issue in the course of their work and can react to it, versus needing to remember it.

In many cases, standardized work is just as simple as that: one line in an electronic form and six steps written in explanation for training new people. The power is in the visibility. Instead of work that is a series of unexamined habits, standardized work has been considered from many angles, written down, and embedded in the environment for all to see.

When standardized work is updated, team leaders are responsible for two actions: making sure that the work environment reflects the new work and is intuitive for the associate and then changing the documentation. In many work cells on the shop floor, we still have poster-sized diagrams of that station's standardized work. But we no longer expect the associate to refer to them for guidance. The charts are for the benefit of team leaders who can see at a glance where associates are in their work cycle, if they are ahead or behind, and take appropriate actions if needed. When engineers make design changes that affect standardized work, they are now responsible for working with the team leader to translate the changes into the work flow and document it.

The next step is to help team leaders create an auditing system, so that they can review every piece of standardized work on a regular basis. In the Netherlands, the team leader on the case-erector line has made auditing a part of his standardized daily work. We hope to expand this practice throughout the organization.

The times I spend in standardized-work mode are now some of my favorite hours in a week. For those hours, I do not need to think about where else I need to be or create an agenda. Information is spoon-fed to me and so, instead of hunting down data or trying to figure out the right questions to ask, I can focus on the information provided and on developing the people who are providing it.

I do hear people say that they do not like the idea of standardized work because they fear it makes them like hamburger flippers—robotic, low-skilled labor. A lot of folks at Lantech have specialized training and years of experience. They do not want to be devalued. So, I tell people—often and repeatedly—that they should not be using their talents and experience to solve the same problems every day. They should be finding and solving new problems. But we cannot get past the old problems until we have standardized work to hold the process steady and give us time to solve the next layer of problems. We need standardized work so that we can stand on the shoulders of problems that have been solved and accumulate competitive advantage.

I remain committed to the WARs and my own standardized work because I see their benefits. These daily conversations make thorny issues visible. Instead of discovering problems late and trying to manage by rumor or third-hand reports—which I find very frustrating—I see exactly what people are doing and how they work. This allows me to have directed, specific conversations with my direct reports and to coach them through issues that arise.

I tell people the goal is to make our problems visible—to bring them to the surface as early as possible—so that we can solve them instead of being surprised by them.

This leads us to how we solve problems.

Chapter 6

Solving the Immediate Problem

The customer on the other end of the line had every reason to be angry. The general manager of a big factory of a brand-name company, he had just taken possession of one of our stretch-wrapping machines. For weeks his engineers had anticipated its arrival, making plans to integrate it into their operations. The delivery day had finally come, but with a whimper instead of a bang.

When they peeled away the cardboard and plastic, his employees discovered parts rattling around in the main electrical box. Screws were loose, and components in the control enclosure had fallen apart in transit. What was wrong with my plant? the general manager wanted to know. It was a good question.

This was in 2007, in the early days of our daily management system when we were doing a lot of experimentation. I pulled Gina and Steve into a meeting on the shop floor and said, "We can't keep sending out machines with quality problems. It's embarrassing us and hurting our brand. So, starting right now, we're not shipping anything—not a single machine—until it has a complete, detailed quality audit by someone other than the folks in final assembly and test."

Gina and Steve just looked at me for a minute. They knew as well as I that this was a kind of heresy. Adherents of the Toyota Production System consider final testing and audits of the finished product *muda*.[18] We should have such well-designed processes, the argument went, that no product could be produced with defects. Any abnormality should be stopped in its tracks. But after more than a decade in search of this perfect state, we found that defects were still making it out the back door.

Finally, Gina broke the silence. Final audit was a time-consuming task, she said. Who could we assign to do it? What about the quality control team? I asked. We had four engineers on that team. Surely, that would be enough people to do a thorough quality check before shipment. Gina shook her head. They were busy, she said.

"Doing what?" I asked testily.

By this time, Bob Morgan had been doing a good job drilling the "go see" message into our heads, so we went to the desk of the quality engineers to see what they were doing. Sure enough, they were all hard at work in front of their computers, managing and reordering the lists of defects. Every problem we had was given a code and sorted by type. They were prioritizing, cataloging new problems, and updating the progress toward solutions on close to 100 old problems. Suddenly, it seemed ridiculous to me. I asked them to stop. This might sound radical, but that was the last time we ever tracked old problems.

Their new job would be in an area just prior to shipping, where they would do a 100% audit on every machine. The audit would focus in particular on recent defects reported in the field by customers and service technicians. Then, they would take a

---

18. Japanese for "waste."

problem that they found, chase down the source of the problem—in the process, not the people—and devise a solution with the area's team leader.

"No more priority lists and defect catalogs," I said. "Find our problems and fix them."

Around the same time, Bob Morgan introduced us to quality loop boards and the idea that a growing number of defects would trip an andon that would help us guard against process erosion. This was like the quality run rates that we established throughout Lantech for the walk-around reviews. The quality team, while auditing every machine prior to shipping, noted how many problems were found per machine. When we had a day where the average number of problems per machine suddenly was higher, we asked, "What was different yesterday?"

One early case I remember clearly. With yesterday's audits still fresh in their minds, the quality team members agreed that a big issue was scratched paint on the top of certain types of machines. The scratch was not on every machine, but it occurred enough to be notable. The team then began speculating about what might have caused it. I held up a hand.

"How about going to look at that process? You think you can do that and report back after lunch?" I asked.

After lunch, an engineer reported that while watching parts being unloaded from the paint booth, he noticed that the padding on one particular paint cart was loose. Sometimes the operator adjusted it before removing the part; sometimes the operator did not and it left a scratch in the fresh paint. We reattached the padding on that part cart, and the issue was solved.

Over the next nine months, as we chased down immediate problems to the source and fixed them, the average number of problems on a Q-Semi machine found at final inspection dropped from seven to one. And then it was less than one per machine.

On the more complex S-Auto machines, average problems dropped from just under 20 per machine to two. Our production lines did less sputtering and stopping and were starting to run smoothly. Instead of daily disasters, we were finding and fixing problems before they snowballed.

From this, I learned an indelible truth: solving the problem that presents itself now is more valuable than finding and attacking the most important problem we have. Solving today's problems— the immediate problems that might seem simple or insignificant— has helped us improve productivity and quality like no other initiative in my 21-year tenure.

Of course, we spent years laying the groundwork before we arrived at that point. Having processes that are set up as one-piece flow is critical to finding and solving problems. If we were still running a lot of batch processing, we would naturally reach for easy work-arounds when we hit a snag instead of uncovering problems. When there is extra inventory, problems get hidden fast. In a one-piece-flow environment, problems are visible and painful—production lines stop, people become idle—so problem solving has real urgency.

This is not to imply, however, that we just set people loose and tell them to solve problems any which way. We have discovered a few rules that help us drive toward root cause, and we are always reminding ourselves to use this simple framework.

- First, go and see. We must be able to see the problem as it occurs, and to watch as the output of a process turns from good to bad, if we hope to move past guesswork.

- Next, create and maintain visibility of the problem-solving process. Be clear about who will do what and when.

- Finally, after a countermeasure is implemented, include a clear plan to guard against backsliding. Any change in a process must contain a method for monitoring that new process. For this, we usually use the structure of the daily management system by choosing a measure or a simple device to make deterioration visible to a team leader during the morning environment walk.

We will illustrate our problem-solving framework a little later in this chapter, but before we go further, I also want to say that, beyond the three rules listed above, I firmly believe there is no single problem-solving method that will work in every part of a business. I have heard lean champions tell their people that if a problem did not have an A3, it could not be solved. Or say that a Six Sigma project is necessary. People argue about whether it should be PDCA or PDSA[19] and how, exactly, a form should be filled out. This kind of rigidity just does not work for us.

A problem with a shortage of parts, for instance, requires a different kind of attention than a problem with an unaccountable drop in accounts receivables. A parts shortage could have originated in a dozen different ways and might involve four departments and an outside supplier. We might have 50 people who have a vested interest in the outcome. Meanwhile, there might be exactly three people in the entire company who understand the computer programs of invoicing in accounts receivable and can investigate the drop in payment performance by customers. So, seeing the problem occur may take a really fast camera for some types of problems, good knowledge of our ERP system for other problems, and artful observation skills for others.

---

19. This is "plan, do, check, act" versus "plan, do, study, and adjust," which is simply two ways of wording the problem-solving cycle popularized by W. Edwards Deming.

Also, while we do not spend time listing and prioritizing our problems company-wide anymore, we still need to have common understandings about where to spend our energy and when to pass information about problems to higher levels of management. This last piece is woven right into the fabric of the daily management system. Instead of having complicated rules—or worse, absolute silence—on when you should tell your boss about a problem, we have a daily, on-going conversation about problems during the walk-around review. During this daily meeting, we talk about new problems, old problems, how we are getting to point-of-cause and proposed fixes, and how we mentor everyone in the best way to dig for the root cause of problems. Since I am not immune from occasionally jumping to solutions, sometimes I am the one being mentored.

As for priorities, I have some simple principles. Whatever is closest to the customer gets our attention first. If a customer in the field has a machine down, that gets solved first. We don't spend a lot of time getting to root cause until we get the customer up and running. Then we look into the systemic issues that might have caused the failure if we have the capacity to do so.

Next on the priority list are the machines in production right now for customers. This is why we begin every walk-around review at shipping, which is just moments away from the customer, and then swim upstream in the process. As leadership walks from shipping to assembly to procurement to engineering to sales, we can bring up the issues that are happening close to the customer and make sure they are getting the appropriate attention from people in engineering or procurement or wherever is appropriate. After all, most problems that surface in final assembly have their origins in engineering or inside sales or one of the other upstream departments we visit.

For instance, let's say there was a machine in final assembly with a custom fence.[20] The elements were supposed to snap together easily but did not. It took the technician longer than expected, so the team leader stepped into the work area and inquired about the problem. They looked at it together but could not make the pieces fit. The team leader moved the technician to different work—in process improvement or training—and called for help from engineering or procurement to get the issue resolved rapidly. In this case, the problem would also be noted on the WAR board.

The leadership walk-around review comes by at 9:20 a.m. If we see the issue is still current on the board, we ask about followup. Either the team leader would report that engineering is working on it now or we would assign someone on the leadership team to follow up personally with engineering when we get there, moments later. That means the person who designed the fencing is there on the floor with the pieces in his hands, working with the technician to fix the problem as soon as possible. An issue like this will probably never require an A3 or team-based problem solving.

When we want to drill down to root cause on an issue, and for guarding against deterioration of processes, we use a quality loop, as introduced in chapter 3. We use this simple what-how-who-when process in two specific ways: to help us unearth hard-to-see problems and to guide people through solving the issues productively.

As a mentoring device, the quality loop is pretty straight-forward. During our walk-around review, if a problem is being discussed, we might ask the team leader to grab a marker, and we talk through each step of the form.

---

20. Large machines usually include a fenced perimeter for safety, to keep employees and forklifts away from moving or sensitive mechanisms. Fences are usually custom designed to fit the conditions of the customer site.

We ask, "What is the problem? Have you seen it? How can you see it? When can you do that? OK, great, write that down."

If people in the area have already seen the problem and want to test a solution, that's what goes on the form instead. Each step of the way, there are time commitments and a person's name attached to each action.

By now, everyone knows the rule: the first step is going to see the problem as it occurs. We do not want any talk about potential solutions in this first step. We do not take actions to affect the process—otherwise known as messing with the crime scene—because the most important first step is to see where the process went from good to bad. First, we simply want to devise ways to get eyes on the situation at the exact right moment.

One problem we've dealt with, for instance, has been belt tracking. The mechanics require a little explanation here. When a load on a pallet is being wrapped for shipping, the load remains in place while the film delivery system—think of this as a large, precisely controlled roll of plastic wrap—moves around it. An arm moves the film delivery system around the load, and a belt moves it up and down to wrap the load from top to bottom.

The problem has often been that the belt that lifts the film dispenser up and down doesn't track true. As the belt moves over a series of rollers, sometimes it would shimmy to the left side of the rollers and other times over to the right. Technicians could generally adjust various components to get the belt back on track, but the adjustments took time and were always different.

When a slot was free on the area's quality loop, the belt-tracking problem was added. In order to see where the process went from good to bad, we needed to identify all the possibilities, working backward through the process.

The belts are set in motion by an electrical motor, a gear reducer, and a metal drum. One end of the belt is attached to the film dispenser and the other end to the drum, which winds up the belt to raise the film dispenser and unwinds to lower it. A programmable logic controller (PLC) governs the motor.

The team working on the problem painstakingly drew a system diagram with every possible variable identified (*see page 84*). This made it easier to methodically investigate every possibility. The system diagram took a while to build, so the area's quality loop sheet noted that they were working on it for several days.

Then the team began digging into each variable and found, for instance, that on machines with a poorly tracking belt, the rollers were all exactly the same. The brackets that held the belt in place were identical on good and bad machines. The weave of the belt was also unchanged. These were not the problem.

But wait. The drum that set the belt in motion did have some variation in shape between good and bad machines. Once the drum shape was corrected, the belt tracked true. Until a few weeks later when it didn't again. The next time it happened, we returned to the meticulous system diagram to help us take that first step into seeing the problem and worked through each of the variables until we found the new root cause.

When we have IT problems, such as unwanted system reboots, where we cannot use a well-placed camera or some other visual method to catch the good/bad divide, we draw system diagrams on flip charts or whiteboards to make the possible issues and errors as visible as possible. This forces us to move logically through each step of a process that is largely hidden from the human eye.

After a solution has been proposed and implemented, we assign someone to watch it for five iterations to ensure the solution is stable. Trouble almost always shows up early, and if someone is watching carefully, we can make adjustments to stabilize the new process or rethink the solution.

System Diagram Sketch for Belt System

Standardized Work

JOB CONTENT	From:	Owner:
	To:	Takt Tim

KEY POINTS ▲   WIP ●

UP ↑

Down ↓

← FDS

Chart

	Revision / Date	
ne:		

QUALITY CHECK ◊   **SAFETY ✛**

System Diagram

Drive Unit with drum

Keeping it simple has become a mantra at Lantech. I am sure that there are companies such as chemical processors where changes in the process are almost impossible to see with the naked eye and require massive amounts of data in order to measure and confirm. The rest of us, I think, have a tendency to get needlessly wrapped up in how many sigmas of deviation a process has when we should be using our creative energy to figure out how to see the process as it goes from good to bad.

We use the quality loop for another kind of *seeing*, as well: to help reveal the problems that might seem small but are eroding the process. For this, the quality loop relies on another daily habit of team leaders throughout Lantech: collecting QCDS[21] data.

Every team leader has a list of measures that fall into the categories of quality, cost, delivery, and safety. Every day the team leader checks in on how their area is doing against the established run rates for these measures. For instance, the leader might start the day with a two-minute safety walk through their area, checking for cleanliness, tripping hazards, guards in place, the presence of the right equipment, etc. Every problem they find is a tick mark on the check sheet. If the run rate is three tick marks or fewer and today's tally is eight, the safety measure goes to red.

For a particular quality measure, they might note the number of quality issues that occurred the day before. For cost and delivery, the leader might note any work that had to be redone and any late deliveries. What's important is the number of issues and how it measures against the running average.

Throughout Lantech, leaders are running daily quick checks against their QCDS measures, looking at everything from price deviations to current skills development matrices to on-time deliveries in their areas. (This system is an evolution of our first

---

21. QCDS: quality, cost, delivery, safety.

WAR board quality indicators, when area leaders picked just two measures, displayed as run rates. The measures on these sheets are rewritten or affirmed every year during strategy deployment sessions to keep them in line with Lantech's focus.)

Every leader knows the running 90-day average of all the area's measures, and these are written on the WAR boards. If any of the day's measures falls outside that average, the number on the board in that area goes from green to red. This is our alert that there is possible deterioration of the process, and we ask what changed in this area yesterday.

Right next to an area's QCDS measures on the walk-around review board there is a quality loop sheet with five possible slots. If there is an open slot and a red QCDS number—which we think of as a tripped andon—with an unknown cause, we will most likely write down the issue and start looking for ways to see where the process went from good to bad.

If a team leader already has all five slots filled with problems on the quality loop sheet, we make sure the tripped andon is not negatively impacting a customer's needs and then we drop it. We figure the problem is likely to come back around in the future, at a time when we have capacity on the quality loop form, and we can catch it then.

That might sound dismissive, but I know that a team cannot attack more than five problems at once. If you have 25 problems on a board, you are not doing much of anything besides noting incremental changes in your 25 problems and hoping to someday get to root cause on one of them. When people have a lot of problems, they tend to develop a desire to list them in a database, analyze their various aspects, and make charts about them. But when we spend time doing that, we are not spending time solving them. In other words, if we get a whole herd of problems on the board, we can do little but manage the herd.

With a finite number, however, we can work toward root cause and implementing fixes that will stick. And, as I have said, solved problems equal increased productivity. Immediacy is a central goal in our problem solving.

While seeing an issue is the critical first step, we encounter a lot of problems where I would say that making it visible to people—communicating the problem, the elements of the investigation, and the results—are a close second in importance. For those issues, we use an A3.

Every WAR board at Lantech is divided into two sides. On the left where we focus on immediate issues and maintaining the current condition, there are quality loop forms. On the right, where we focus on improvement and longer-term projects, A3s typically dominate.

Because A3s are often used for big projects such as strategy deployment, we will go into greater depth on how we use them in chapter 11. For now, I will say that A3s are a teaching tool just as much as they are a project management tool. Like the quality loop form, we use A3s to teach people how to work methodically through the problem-solving process. We also teach them to keep track of big projects by using a key task monitor.

Instead of explaining these tools point by point in an abstract way, let's move on in our story to a time when we can see them in action. During a recent crisis that rocked Lantech to its core, these tools and the daily management system showed us how change— very necessary change—was possible.

Chapter 7

A People Crisis

Amidsized company such as Lantech does not have much extra padding. We feel market swings early, long before they show up in the newspapers, and so sometimes we get surprised. When the local economy started rising up out of the Great Recession, for instance, we were still focused pretty hard on survival skills and our new insourcing efforts. Head down in the work like that, I was blindsided when we started losing skilled people in 2014 to other opportunities.

My dad and I both prided ourselves on creating a family feeling in the company. We mostly hired good, inexperienced people and taught them a trade—often, more than one—and kept them with us for decades. We knew people's families. We knew their troubles and joys. People who were in good standing after a year at Lantech were more likely to be with us for five years. And we rarely lost employees after their fifth anniversary.

In the past, the way we competed for employee retention was with market-based wages and the loyalty that comes from a family culture. When we had problems on the shop floor or in the offices, we pitched in and worked out solutions together. This was great in 2008 and 2009, when we were all working hard to save the company and implement a new management system.

We discovered, however, that there is a dark side to standardization. We used to stand shoulder to shoulder with our associates, asking them for suggestions on solving tricky problems. As our systems became habits and work processes stabilized and required less change, we stopped asking for our associates' opinions about their jobs and the Lantech environment.

By 2014 and 2015, senior leaders were focusing on growth in the insourcing business. Leaders and managers in the main plant started to fall back on shortcut problem solving. They gave answers instead of soliciting ideas. Some of our associates—especially those in well-oiled and standardized work cells—were looking at a future of performing the same set of perfectly rational and intuitive work steps day in and day out, and it was unappealing.

Three other developments made the situation even worse. Baby boomers were hitting retirement age, and a good number of our long-term employees were dreaming of good fishing and a slower pace. Meanwhile, the millennial generation that was just graduating high school had been learning many things but was not tinkering with tools in shop class. We were graduating fewer and fewer kids who were prepared for or excited about industrial or technical jobs.

Meanwhile, manufacturing in Louisville was growing at four times the rate of Kentucky and 10 times as fast as the national manufacturing rate. Big car companies and appliance makers moved in or expanded, and they could offer top dollar in salaries and benefits to trained welders and electricians and machine operators. Suddenly, if one of our folks ended the week feeling a little disgruntled or wondering whether they really had a future at Lantech, all they needed to do was open the Sunday paper to see fresh opportunities.

So now, while process problems were on top of my agenda, it was starting to dawn on me that I had a people crisis. By this time, the snowball had already started building up speed. In 2014, Lantech's pay rate was average for manufacturing in the region, according to the data we could gather. And then new manufacturing concerns started coming in and paying a good bit more to attract the already-trained talent in our shops.

We might have an employee or two get fed up with us and leave. Then they would tell their friends back at Lantech how much more they were making at their new jobs, and we might lose another half dozen associates. Then we have two team leaders who no longer have time to manage people and situations because they are back filling in on the assembly line or the conveyor shop. Problems got ignored; people were stressed. So we lost a few more people.

There were months when we lost eight or nine people. A new company in town poached nearly our entire electrical panel shop. For a company our size, we were hemorrhaging. Of course, we immediately did the obvious thing and recalibrated our pay rate. But considering some of the big brand-name manufacturers that had moved into town, I knew we could not compete on hourly rates and benefits alone. We needed to launch a fresh effort to develop people faster and find a way back to that sense of Lantech as a family place—a place you don't want to leave.

I can still remember taking a deep breath one day and thinking to myself, "OK. Step one: go and see the problem. We need to find out why we're losing people—from the source."

Typically, HR did informal exit interviews with people. In the course of that interview, we might ask a question about what we could improve at Lantech. But let's face it: most of the time, a happily retiring person develops quick amnesia about anything negative. And it's nice to let people exit on a high note, to ride off happy into the sunset, even if it fails to yield useful information.

In 2014, however, we started having people leave younger and with a frown. I asked HR to step in and start doing more formal exit interviews and in particular to ask about dissatisfaction. Then I realized we better start talking to folks long before they gave notice, so we refocused on new hires. We developed standardized questionnaires for people after 30 days, 90 days, and one year from being hired. A manager (sometimes me) always sits down with the new hires somewhere with privacy but near the person's workplace. Then we talk through the questions instead of having the associate write it out. We're hoping for a conversation and always looking for that little extra bit of intelligence.

Pretty soon, a pattern started to emerge. Associates in their first 30 days mostly gave gushing reviews. They had received training; they had the right tools and a clean place to work. People were helpful and friendly, new hires reported.

At 90 days, folks started to hedge. They would start off with an excuse like, "Well, my team leader is really busy. I know that. I just wish I knew how I screwed up. I mean, does it really matter if I'm two minutes late?"

From responses like that, we knew that we were not communicating some key points. If people did not understand why it was important to be on time, they were obviously not clear on how their work tied into the whole. More important, they knew how they got in trouble but did not know how to get out of it. Associates who made it to the one-year-anniversary interview were not settled in the way they used to be.

Stressed as we were with that unusual turnover, we were hesitant to layer on another initiative or program to fix our problem. Fortunately, Bob Morgan once again came to the rescue, offering a simple tool that became part of the daily management system: the STAMP board (*see example at right*).

Example of a STAMP Board

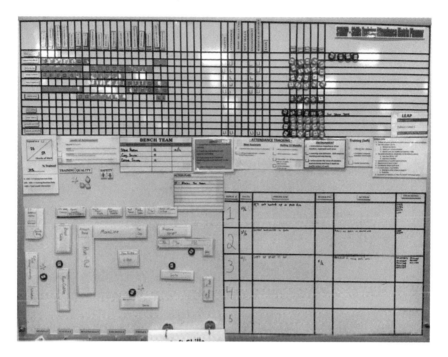

The Skills, Training, Attendance Matrix Planner (STAMP) board is a large whiteboard of our usual home-improvement-store construction. Placed in each work area, it shows all associates at a glance how they are doing toward their goals. Their progress toward acquiring technical skills, soft skills, and their current attendance record are laid out for everyone to see. There are columns that show how well they demonstrate safety procedures and work through problems.

In short, all of our expectations are on that board. As long as the boards stay current and team leaders hold their morning meetings in front of that board, we believe we will be able to avoid the kind of closed-door performance reviews that result in surprises, miscommunication, and early exits.

When designing the boards with Bob Morgan, we worked to make all of our expectations visible and achievable. For the technical side, that meant looking at our jobs and breaking them down into levels of achievement. Some of this was already in place, of course, but we needed it to be formal.

So we put together a team that identified the eight skills of manufacturing, such as assembly, welding, electrical wiring, etc. Then we broke each skill down into a number of levels, from novice to expert. Welders, for instance, progress through six levels, and there are specific competencies and pay levels attached to each level. This helped us create a common understanding of skills required for advancement in many job categories.

Soft skills include areas such as performance feedback training, in which the associate learns how to give and receive feedback on performance in a positive manner. This is the first skill every new employee learns in a training session with HR.

Team leaders receive special training in listening skills, how to maintain and enhance self-esteem, and how to respond with empathy. "Sharing thoughts, feelings, and rationale" is also a unit of training. I am still learning and relearning that one.

When Bob brought us the STAMP board, it seemed like an awful lot of information to corral, but it turns out that it can be amazingly simple and straightforward. Steve Clifford did a lot of the initial STAMP rollout to all of our production areas in January 2016, and, since he is using the boards every day with his production-line leaders, I will lean on him for the details.

"Before we put these boards together, we had a lot of discussions with people, and I have to admit I was surprised by what we heard," Steve says now in his easy drawl. "I kept thinking, 'We're paying X amount of money for this position. It's a good job in a clean area. We all get along. So why are people leaving?'

"Finally looking at the interviews, I think we all realized that we had lots of discipline around quality, cycle time, and attendance. But we did not have a clear way to show people how they could progress. We were all stick and no carrot. It was not respectful to the associates. We needed to show them greener pasture, so they would feel better about their futures and the company."

Since STAMP is a lean tool, it is driven by data, visible to all, and designed to be discussed and updated on a daily basis. Team leaders meet with their teams—usually between six and 10 people —in the morning to discuss the day's work. Attendance is updated on the board along with skills training. Team leaders acknowledge a person's progress toward mastering a skill with a series of marks that ultimately form a square. It begins as an "I" for completing instruction, then an "L" when they have learned the skill, and then a "U" when they demonstrate understanding. The final bar across the top that completes the square indicates consistency.

Information from STAMP becomes part of the team leader's QCDS metrics, which is summarized and rolled up in the morning walk-around review. When all of us are speaking the same language and looking for the same information every day, I have found that it is much easier to look deep into the details of my company that I might not see otherwise, such as whether entry-level employees are receiving adequate training this week. And the associates also know what they are expected to learn and how they can achieve their own goals.

"When we rolled out the STAMP boards, we found ourselves having some interesting conversations," Steve says. "In one work cell, for instance, there was a guy who had a history of bad attendance issues. So I'm up there telling them about the attendance column and how we expect associates in good standing to have three tardy arrivals or less and 30 hours maximum of unplanned absence in a rolling 12-month period.

"I can see this guy shaking his head as I'm talking, and sure enough, as soon as I'm finished, he says, 'Now wait a minute. Are you telling me I've got to have 30 hours or less in unplanned absences before I can be promoted?' I said, 'Yes, that's exactly what I'm saying.' And you know, in the three months since then, he has not missed one hour of work. He knows if he can keep his record clean until June something, he is promotable. So he has a goal.

"Really, there have been several instances of this kind of thing happening. It's not like people were not trying to do the right thing. They just were not clear on what the right thing was. We can't keep clear on everyone's goals when we're having just one or two rushed, private conversations a year," Steve says.

Having squares in all the right boxes, everyone knows, means the individual is promotable. If a team leader sees that someone is losing ground on certain skills, such as ignoring safety training and being caught without a seat belt while driving a truck, they might have a talk with the associate while taking a mark or two off of the employee's "safety" square. At the same time, the leader tells the associate how to get back to the "promotable" category, which in this case might be showing that they wear their seat belt consistently for the next month.

For Steve, the fact that his team leaders are having those daily conversations means there is a lot more clarity. People know what they need to do in order to further their careers, and conversations are less awkward. Receiving training, showing off some soft skills, showing up on time—all of it adds up to some clear stepping-stones toward raises and promotions.

"As a team leader, I used to avoid hard conversations that I knew I needed to have," Steve says. "And the longer you avoid it, the worse it gets. It's like ice forms over the relationship, and then you have to break that ice in order to have the conversation. What

I'm hoping this board does is keep the ice from forming. It's like daily feedback on job performance, at a glance."

At this point, it probably sounds like all of our efforts are aimed at people on the shop floor. That is not entirely true. Since many of our employees and most of our new hires are in the production area, that is where we have focused our energy with the STAMP rollout. We have a version of the boards in our professional offices, as well, but this is not a focused initiative like it is on the shop floor.

In our support offices, we have found that the morning walk-around reviews offer people-development opportunities that are better calibrated to that environment. After all, our support offices have completely different issues. From one office to the next—from information technology to engineering to accounting— teams are small and stable. Jobs are so specialized that a much bigger problem for us was that many people were stuck in silo-type thinking.

The IT team, for instance, used to talk to each other a lot about computer software and the advantage of one security system over another but rarely engaged other departments. Our biggest people-development challenge was getting these folks out of their silos, capable of communicating about their work clearly, and working together for the common good.

When I think about the people-development tactics that worked for us in support offices, I realize how much our sense of responsibilities has changed over the past few years. Jeff Collins, for instance, is on our IT team. He has been with Lantech for 12 years, and before the new management system was in place, he liked his job just fine. He had good relationships and easy access to his boss and his boss's boss. They had long, friendly meetings discussing new technologies or how to make use of social media and such.

Jeff was not a fan when the walk-around reviews started up in 2008. Once a week, on Fridays, he was expected to present his work to a senior management team. It was supposed to take only three minutes or so to tell the group what IT was working on and whether there were any significant issues. But, with all those senior leaders squeezed into his office, all with varying degrees of computer knowledge, it always took longer and was more stressful than had been billed.

"In the beginning, I didn't know how to talk to them. And I couldn't imagine how they could help me do my job," Jeff says.

In fact, we all quickly discovered that understanding the issues in IT would not be simple. Jeff tried to explain things to the group with spreadsheets filled with numbers, but that did not help. We asked him to draw pictures instead. He felt silly about it, but he drew pictures of the plant with bold lines leading to the Internet service provider, more lines representing the firewalls and such. Other people on his team would look at his drawings and remind him of a system reboot that they did here, a new program installation there. As his drawings took on more detail, we all started asking better questions of the process and Jeff got a lot more comfortable with the senior leaders crowded into his office. After a year or so, he got to know people from all over the building. He even started to see the value in those Friday meetings.

"Ten years ago, if we had new hardware or software to introduce, we used to have lots of individual conversations with people that did not add all that much value," Jeff says. "We were never sure what people really understood and whether we were serving them. It was exhausting. Now, I can introduce something like that in 15 minutes on a Friday, mostly because everyone is aware that this was coming and they have all had input into our final decisions."

The best part of Jeff's development, as far as I'm concerned, has been in the way his focus has changed. He used to have a pretty insular point of view. His circle of colleagues was small and like-minded; his customers were all Lantech employees.

Then, in 2015, he was chatting with Alex Verret, the head of our technical service department. Alex was working on an idea to help service technicians find and fix problems in our machines before the customer was affected or even knew about a problem. Alex talked to Jeff about what was possible, and they started talking through some ideas. Alex was fired up to start putting ideas into reality, but Jeff paused. This was really outside of his usual work, and he had many projects demanding his attention.

On Friday, senior leadership was all there in Jeff's office again asking him for the usual update. He mentioned Alex's idea and that he had some competing priorities and asked for guidance. I asked Jeff about the content of his other work. He had scheduled an upgrade of laptops in the coming weeks that was going to take much of his time.

Conversations like this are a gift. It was the perfect opening for me to underline the importance of that service-department project. Having machines in the field talk back to us was actually the first step of a longer-range strategy that was just taking shape.

When a company buys a Lantech stretch wrapper, it is purchasing the ability to secure a load of products for shipment. This is no small thing. Merchandise lost or destroyed in transit around the globe adds up to billions in waste every year. That means supply chains interrupted, unnecessary garbage, and cost in the system. Ensuring safe shipments is a competitive advantage.

The question is, do our clients really want a machine? No. They want a load secured for shipment. So, we were imagining selling a service that guaranteed uptime on our stretch wrappers, creating loads that would not shift or spill in transit. Instead of a machine, we could sell a subscription service, I told Jeff. To make it work, we would need to have complete visibility into our machines operating in customers' plants. It was an interesting question, how to achieve this.

On that Friday, Jeff saw the trajectory of Lantech changing and began recalibrating his own priorities to meet the needs of the company. Updated laptops could wait a few weeks without significant cost or trouble, he said. Getting our machines in the field to report back to the mothership via the Internet was a far more compelling project.

I began telling this story about Jeff, but I can see now that it is also about my own personal development. Some nine years after we began our walk-around reviews, I am not the same leader. Even my vision of what I want to be, how I want to act, has changed.

Back in the day, I thought of myself as the wildly creative guy. I came back from New York with big ideas and full of fire. Within a few years, I had worked in just about every facet of the company and had more breadth of information than anyone. I had heard that it was good to let go and allow others to lead, of course. But I tried that with the president of North American operations and his "accountability" initiative and found it a near disaster. By the time Bob Morgan came to help us, I was a little unpredictable and given to micromanaging. It was not a great combination.

In his steady, sure way, Bob taught me to become a teacher and mentor. Bob taught us that when teaching someone how to do a task, we should break it into smaller chunks and allow a person to learn a little at a time. Gaining confidence along with competence is important when learning a new skill, and Bob taught me to support people as they learned, to help them do it correctly, and to explain why we do things a certain way. Someone who has learned a skill should also turn around and teach it, in order to ingrain the knowledge.

In becoming a teacher and conducting those walk-around reviews, I learned how much more value I could bring to the company by being systematic and predictable, by asking questions instead of shooting off answers. And I have learned to put the process ahead of my own ego.

Eight years earlier, I probably would not have known that Jeff, an IT network administrator, was facing a question about how to prioritize his time that would have a direct impact on our future. If I did, I would have told him what to do and he would have left that conversation feeling a little less capable, a little less engaged in the work. It is doubtful that I would have stopped long enough to explain my thinking around the subject.

The old me never could have imagined showing up at the same place every day, or even once a week, and asking the same questions like a film actor hitting the mark in take after take. But I find myself completely engaged with the process. Even when Gina, Steve, or Ryan has to remind me not to jump to solutions, I enjoy myself on those walk-around reviews.

I also recognize that I am not the best practitioner of the walk-around review. There is an art to those morning huddles, to supporting the work in a way that leaves people feeling personally supported. So, for the next chapter, I'm going to introduce Gina, Steve, and Ryan—the real pros—and have them offer up lessons they have learned on conducting the morning WAR. There is much to learn about this particular art of WAR.

Chapter 8

The Art of the WAR[22]

When Bob Morgan first taught us about the walk-around review, there was one point that he made sure we all understood: there was more than one way we could really mess this up. The WAR was both sand castle maintenance and people development for everyone at every level. It took the very personal act of coaching, put it in a public setting, and set it on a strict time clock.

Do it wrong, Bob warned, and there would be a lot of ticked-off team leaders without the support they needed—just more work to do and "solutions" to problems that were not fully understood. If we started shooting from the hip, we could kick our sand castle apart.

In the beginning, we stopped after almost every area's review and asked each other whether we actually helped the team leader. And nearly every morning for that first year, one us would loop back around and try to straighten out whatever misperception we had left behind. We all carried clipboards in the beginning, and Gina made up some cards for us with reminders on how to behave. It sounds silly, but it really helped.

---

22. I have heard Bob Morgan say that the Chinese military treatise from the fifth century BC, *The Art of War* by Sun Tzu, is the greatest management book ever written. Here, however, I am referring to the skills and empathy needed to have a successful walk-around review practice.

Taped to the metal clip at the top of the board, these cards displayed the rules of the WAR, and they saved our bacon more than once. The rules gave us plenty of clearance to correct each other and ourselves when we were wandering off the path. This is my memory of the rules:

The Rules of the WAR

1. Do not solve what is not ours to solve.
2. Do grab and own what is ours to decide or solve.
3. Don't give solutions to what we have not seen with our own eyes.
4. Don't judge, just guide.
5. Don't embarrass a manager in front of direct reports.

Steve and Gina have different memories of the rules. We have all looked through every file we can think of but have not found those cards. So I have asked them, plus relative newcomer Ryan Bryant, to share the rules they live by now. For Steve and Gina, this amounts to eight years of accumulated wisdom from daily walks. Ryan brings fresh eyes to the topic. I will introduce each of them but then hang back and let them share what they've learned.

Gina McIntosh is director of operations. All of manufacturing, procurement, materials, application engineering, aftermarket parts and service, and documentation report to her in the Louisville operation. She is my steady right hand.

Gina was studying to be a farm animal veterinarian in the early 1980s when family needs intervened and she came home to help out her mother and little sister and quickly got a job with us at Lantech. She started out as a materials handler, became a parts clerk, did quality assessment in the machine shop, processed warranties, and was made a team leader in five years. We won her loyalty, Gina says, by being generous with training and always showing her growth possibilities. Her presence on the WAR is a constant reminder as to the real value of developing our people. This is what she has learned:

"My number-one rule when we approach a WAR board is to remember who is in control. The team leader owns that area. I might be higher on the chain of command, but that person is in control, and we are there only to support the leader and the area. That means if the WAR board is showing all green and there are no business issues, we move on. I never want to be in the position of holding someone up who has an area well in hand.

"If there are problems, we are careful in how we react. First, we are not there to solve problems. We are there to facilitate problem solving. The team leader might need a decision or approval, or we might need to talk them through the problem-solving process.

"The key in these situations is asking nonjudgmental questions. Maybe you think the person hasn't really tried to work through the problem. But you don't want to announce that. We don't ask, 'So, have you tried to problem solve?' Instead we say, 'Where are you in the problem-solving process? Do you have a systems diagram yet?' We don't want to assume they haven't done it. We want to assume that they've already done or are just about to do the right thing.

"Another thing to watch is how we respond to red flags on a WAR board. It can be hard to be neutral and calm. Our natural reaction might be, 'Shoot. What's wrong now?' But we don't want to say that. We have to train ourselves to embrace problems, to see the color red as an opportunity. Think of those team leaders, standing at their WAR boards with a public display of their problems. They are watching us really close to see whether we mean what we say about problems being opportunities and defects being in the process and not the people.

"Jim and Steve laugh at me because I've got an obvious 'tell.' When I get a little upset or frustrated, my ears turn bright red. I'm fairly pale, so it's hard to miss. I've worked hard on changing my attitude about problems, but sometimes my ears still go red. And the last thing I want to do is stand there with my ears all red, pretending like nothing is wrong. So sometimes, the best thing you can do is cut short a conversation at the board, thank the team leader, and circle back around later.

"In fact, knowing when to stop asking questions can be just as important as anything else. It rarely happens now, but back in the beginning, we were often told that the solution to a problem was 'coaching.' Team leaders might tell us, 'We had this problem, so I coached the associate about it.' Well, most times, that's just blaming the associate and not looking at the real problem.

"So, I might ask, 'Is there someone new in the area?' If there is not, I would probably ask, 'What do you think about an experienced person having this issue? Has something changed? The tools? The lighting?' If a person digs in and gets stubborn, we have learned to cut it off quick. Nobody wants too much coaching in public.

"These days, it usually doesn't take long for a team leader to see that they've tagged the solution by blaming the associate. I don't need to get all horrified that they've done it. I just need them to start thinking a little different. We're all used to the process now and what the questions will be, so I spend less time circling back to coach and more time digging into underlying process issues.

"Just this morning, for instance, I was at the WAR board in sales, where their status was red because there was an uptick in the number of quotes that needed to be written compared with the

90-day average. Meanwhile, one associate was out on medical leave, and someone else was traveling. There were more quotes and fewer people to work through them. They had a plan laid out on how to handle the volume change, but the underlying problem that emerged as we talked was that they really did not understand their run rate. Not all quotes take the same time to write, so an average of an average (a run rate calculated assuming that every quote every day requires the same amount of work) could be misleading. The question I wanted to ask was 'If you don't know how long it takes to write the quotes in today's queue, how can you know whether there are enough people to complete the work?'

"I did not ask that question. Instead I asked the team leader how he had identified the difference between quotes that were ready to work and those that were stalled in need of more information. I then asked about the percentage of simple versus complex quotes and how long it might take to write each kind.

"By consistently drawing attention back to the process, the team leader was able to figure out that he actually had fewer workable quotes that day than he thought. And considering how many of them were fairly simple, he would be able to help out, and his team could finish the work without breaking a sweat. He and his team also understood they needed to work a little more on calculating the run rate, looking at the time it takes to write different categories of quotes rather than just counting the number of quotes in the queue.

"You know, very early on in the process Jim asked for my feedback about how he was doing on the WAR. He listened to what I said and respected it. That had a big influence on me. Now, I make a point of asking my direct reports for feedback on how I'm doing. From that, I know that I sometimes miss opportunities to recognize folks, to praise them when they've done a good job. I'm working on that."

Steve Clifford came to work at Lantech as an assembler in the 1980s and proceeded to work his way through nearly all of the different jobs in production. Now, as production manager and a member of our WAR team from the beginning, Steve can put himself in the shoes of just about every operator.

He knows well the role of team leaders, too. Every morning, he conducts his own WAR throughout the plant and then stands at his production board and reports to the senior-leadership WAR. He knows what it feels like to be in every role. That easy-going empathy that Steve displays has been invaluable. But knowing a lot about how a process works can trip us up, too. Here is how he describes the lessons he learned:

"For me, the number-one rule is still do not use this time for solving problems. And it can be really difficult not to correct people. Let's say a quality issue comes up. Maybe someone put something together wrong. It's really hard not to offer the solution. For me, I have to keep reminding myself that I have been away from the work for years now. I don't know everything.

"We know that the first thing we want people to do is go and see the issue. But we are not there to coach folks on what they should do first. So we try to ask open-ended questions as much as possible—or questions that will lead the team leader back toward step one in problem solving. I might ask the team leader, 'Hmm, what tool is the associate supposed to use? Where is it now? Where does the associate pick it up from?'

"At some point in this series of questions, the team leader will not know the answer and hopefully will come to the conclusion that they need to go and see what happens exactly when the process goes from good to bad. We don't want them to jump to solutions, just to tell us the next step.

"When listening to team leader reports, I key in on words like 'probably' and 'I think.' Those words are signs that he or she might not have laid eyes on the work. If they don't know for sure, they need to go look. The words I really want to hear are, 'Guess what I saw?' And, 'My next step is …'

"If I was training someone to come on a walk-around review, the big three directions I would offer are: listen carefully, don't take away problems that are better solved in the area, and don't offer solutions.

"Listening comes first, and it is not necessarily what managers are trained to do. You really need to train yourself to keep your mouth closed and pay attention to what a person is saying. Next, we all have this tendency to take a problem off of someone's hands. But really, most problems are better solved in place. That's why we don't offer solutions or take the problem away; we ask open-ended questions instead.

"Now, I visit seven areas in production every single morning. And I am putting forth effort at every stop, asking open-ended questions, trying to do the right thing. And then I roll up all of that information, and then I stand at my WAR board and report to the leadership WAR. So then I'm on the other side.

"One of the most frustrating things about being on the other side of the discussion is that you stand there and get pelted with questions about what you did and did not do. Some people pride themselves on asking tough questions. It can feel pretty judgmental. And then someone will try to soften it with a qualifying statement like, 'You know what I'm talking about? I'm sure you got it.' It can beat you down a little bit.

"So I try to be aware of that, too. Questions can be perfectly legitimate, but questions, by their very nature, can put people on the defensive. People can end up feeling like their bosses think they don't know what they're doing. So, our questions need to be thoughtful. At the same time, we need to caution new team leaders about growing a little bit of a thick skin. People can end up feeling like they're getting drilled. It's not personal, but folks need to be aware that they might end up feeling like that.

"Here's what I tell people: in a lean environment, you do not want folks in a zone of comfort. In a comfort zone, they're not improving things. Their minds are not working. They are not being challenged. I remember being a production-line team leader in the comfort zone and just being exhausted every day because my mind was not working at full speed. You can see it when a person switches to cruise control. I want to challenge that person because, basically, I want everyone to be in the zone of tension. That's where people are really engaged, and that's when it is fun to be in the work.

"If a person is pushed too hard and gets overwhelmed, they can hit the zone of terror. That's where I back off. If you really listen to a person every day, you can see where they are at.

"For me, doing the same walk-around review every day, carrying around my metrics board, filling in the zeros and ones, I can fall back into the mind-numbing zone of comfort pretty easily. To avoid that, I try to challenge people, to focus on development. Bob Morgan reminds me that the work I do is not about the ugly board I carry to record everyone's status or the markers I use and all the ones and zeros. This is all about making sure our condition is maintained so that we can have a base to improve from. People development is what keeps it interesting.

"And I include myself in that people development. I could do a much better job of acknowledging personal accomplishments. I could say 'good work.' It wasn't the way I was brought up, so it's hard for me to do. On the farm, everybody has jobs, and you just get it done or we don't eat. We don't go around thanking each other for doing chores. I'm still trying to move myself beyond that mind-set."

Ryan Bryant came to Lantech in 2008 as a mechanical engineer, just in time for the Great Recession. We kept him safe from the layoff by moving him from engineering to purchasing, where his job was to find cost savings. Now the manager of purchasing, Ryan became known early on for working hard to show his WAR board as all green all the time and for having quick answers to every problem. He was known for saying, "We're good here. I got it." We tried to explain to him that we needed to see problems in order to understand what was happening. He said, "We're all green here."

Hoping to broaden his perception of the daily management process, we encouraged him to join us for once-a-week walk-around reviews in 2014. He was quiet at first, but within a few months he found his stride and discovered the value of getting intelligence from the front line. Now, Ryan is on the daily leadership WAR and has become a rising star in the management system. He is a relative newcomer, but I value his perspective. Here is his story:

"One thing that was difficult to get used to is that no two WAR boards look alike. Everyone puts their own information up there and uses it in a way that is most useful to their area. I learned that each way was valid, but it took some getting used to.

"Doing this every day helps. I got used to the way that different areas present information and what 'red' means and how to react. And I've learned to be consistent, to stick to the principles of problem solving instead of trying to solve the actual problem. I'm careful about not stepping on toes because, in the end, we want them to solve their own problems.

"I know what it feels like to be standing at my WAR board answering Jim's and Gina's detailed questions about why I chose to do one thing or another. It's the reason I always wanted to show my status as green or to reassure them that my red issues were not important. I wanted them to know that I had the area in control. But that wasn't what they were asking.

"It got a lot easier for me when I realized that they were looking for specific information. If purchasing was showing a red status because a supplier's delivery was late, for instance, they just wanted to know why it was late and whether it would happen again. As long as I called the supplier and had that information before the morning review, they were satisfied. I learned to ask standardized questions of the suppliers in situations like late or missing deliveries.

"Still, I was surprised that they wanted to know those minor details. And I remember feeling micromanaged. So now, when I'm on the other side of the WAR, I like to ask questions a little differently. Instead of asking a team leader what he or she will do about a situation causing a red status, I try to think about how the problem might affect another functional area and ask whether the team leader has alerted that other area. I still find out whether the team leader is on top of the situation; it just feels more respectful.

"I have also learned that there are signs when the WAR isn't going well. Like, the team leader will speak to multiple issues instead of going methodically through the board and touching on the red/green conditions. We do not need to hear about every little detail that's on the WAR board. We need to save our time and attention for any areas showing red.

"There are really three things we want to know at every stop. Are you set up for success today—meaning, are you staffed properly? Are you maintaining the current condition? Are there any business issues that leadership needs to be aware of?

"And I listen for problems that may stem from another area, like purchasing. That's how I can help—knocking down barriers that team leaders encounter.

"The thing I really like about this method is helping people to solve problems. Like, if I show up in the afternoon to follow through on an issue and I help someone get their head around a problem they are trying to solve, the next time I show up in that area, I am welcomed because they know I'm going to help."

———————————

As you can see, I'm proud of Gina, Steve, and Ryan. Each of them has pulled me aside after a WAR stop and addressed the way I asked a question or directed me away from firing off the quick answer, so I know they are paying attention. They are the reason that I felt comfortable cutting back on my own leadership WAR schedule after about five years. I still participate twice a week and keep a sharp eye out for process erosion. With that, I feel confident that the sand castle is well maintained, and knowing that, I can focus more time on improvement.

Chapter 9

Rushing Improvement

So far I have described a lot of improvements we made at Lantech. But here is where we need to make an important distinction. Technically, we were not really *improving*; we were *maintaining*.

We were creating better margins, more reliable quality, and less costly operations by halting deterioration and returning processes to their historic performance levels. That is the work of maintaining. It helped us achieve better, faster production more reliably than anything else we had done. But I was still eager for the next step.

I remembered improvement work and the old days of the kaizen blitz as an exciting time. Back in the 1990s, teams of people were going out onto the factory floor or into work processes in the office to make change for the better nearly every week. We were empowered to dream up improvements and make them into reality in just four days. It was so dynamic that it took us a long time to notice that, after the first several years of structural changes, most improvements did not stick and the big money savings did not materialize on the bottom line. In some ways, it was like we had a 10-year sugar rush before crashing with the realization that improvements weren't sustainable.

The founders of TPS could have predicted our problem. Eiji Toyoda, Taiichi Ohno, Kikuo Suzumura, and Fujio Cho said that without standardized work and process stability there could be no kaizen (improvement). They said this often and emphatically, and it largely fell on deaf ears outside of Toyota.

I was not anxious to go back to those days of a shifting, flimsy foundation, but I still wanted to get into the improvement phase. Bob Morgan cautioned me to stick with maintaining, where there was still much work to be done. But I could not resist. And the experiences we have had in the United States and Europe have at least helped illustrate the distinction between the two phases.

An important difference between *maintain* and *improve* phases is evident in how we arrange problem-solving work. Problem solving of the kind discussed in chapter 6 mostly belongs to maintenance. A simple way to think of it is this: we solve problems in order to restore and maintain the current condition; we improve in order to permanently change the current condition for the better.

When collecting QCDS (quality, cost, delivery, safety) data every morning and comparing the 90-day average run rate to yesterday's events, team leaders are looking for signs of process erosion no matter how small. When they find it, they create a new entry on a quality loop form in order to run down root cause and correct the problem. This is the way we shore up the sand castle walls and create a more stable environment.

The improvement work that Bob finally—and a little reluctantly—taught us has been used to create change. When we needed to prepare for changes to products or processes, or when we are working on larger initiatives to build our capabilities, such as insourcing the manufacture of fabricated parts, we needed different tools.

Since the work of larger initiatives usually involves teams and longer time frames, we use A3s supplemented by key task monitors (KTMs) to help us break down the work steps so we can manage them as standardized work. The KTMs guide us to clearly define the improvement project's work steps and assign a clear time element for each step. Using and regularly reviewing our KTMs gives us an andon system to alert management when work steps are not completed on schedule. This is not so much an accountability tool as it is a management communication tool.

To see this system in action, we can go to February 2015, when it was clear that our rate of employee turnover in production was creating significant skill gaps. Plus, the turnover itself was a sign of lower morale than we thought we had. Where this was most evident was in the work cells that make the Q-Semi. We build 10 of these semiautomatic, turntable stretch wrappers every day. This is where new employees usually begin their careers with Lantech.

Adam Barr, the production-line leader, and Steve Clifford set out to tackle the training problem and developed an A3 titled Manufacturing Readiness (*see page 118*). They began with the problem statement: *Lack of quality training does not provide a sense of growth and skill development.*[23]

We had been training new associates, of course. We showed exactly what to do: how to wire a motor, tighten a setscrew, make sure wires are terminated correctly, and do it all in the required time frame. The problem was we seemed to be telling people that this is what they could look forward to at Lantech: decades of completing a narrow range of tasks with specific instructions in tight time frames. It seemed like a limited and dispiriting future.

---

23. This is not a perfect example of an A3 problem statement in that it assumes the solution is training. A better statement might have been, "Manufacturing associates are leaving because they do not see personal growth opportunities at Lantech." I have decided to let it stand without correcting it because the truth is more important than perfection. We are still working to make our A3 process perfect; we just aren't quite there.

The A3 for Manufacturing Readiness

PROJECT TITLE: Mfg. Readiness (Parent)   **A3 PROPOSED**

PREPARED BY: Steve C. / Adam

1. BUSINESS ISSUE/NEED (THE "PROBLEM")

- Lack of quality training does not provide a sense of growth and skill development.

2. DELIVERABLE/VALUE

- Improved associate morale by providing the ability to grow within the organization, while being taught a skill.

3. CURRENT CONDITION

- Training assoc on what to produce but don't describe how elect./mech things work.
- Many of current hires don't have much if any mechanical appt.
  - Basic hand tools useage / understanding.

WORK REQUEST Task Level A3

B.

DATE: 2/5/15   **REV DATE:**   **REV NUMBER:**

4. HOW TO INVESTIGATE AND GET THIS DONE

- Develop fixturing to aid in training.
- Build work tables to hold assembly aids
- Develop training outline. Task / Condition / Standard (Assessmen
- Use Mfg std practices as training guideline
- Establish different levels of training matching production levels.
  - Pulleys, sheaves / reducers / motors / set screws / etc. (Prod. 1)
- Familiarization training on F.D.S. (Heartbeat of the machine)
- Develop transition plan from training to work cell assignment
- Develop training focused on LEAN. 1 piece flow / Intuitive environment / Terminology.

5. FUTURE CONDITION

ituck

- An associate more skilled and confident to safely deliver a quality product.

6. VERIFICATION

- Noticeable improved retention rate.

MEAP

Step two of the A3 states the intended deliverable. In this case: *Improve associate morale by providing the ability to grow within the organization while being taught or developing a skill.*

Step three is, of course, a statement of the current condition. In this instance we had been compiling the results of many exit interviews for months as well as observing the changing attitudes and aptitudes of new hires.

Steve says, "One guy I remember in particular. He came into Lantech looking to learn a skill, and we trained him to roll steel. He was doing well, but he wasn't all that happy. He told me, 'I want to sit down at the supper table at the end of the day and tell my family what I'm doing and feel good about that.'

"It dawned on us that people wanted a bigger picture. They wanted to know that they were learning machining or electrician skills and how it related to the product. They wanted context for their labor."

So, what they wrote for current condition on the A3 was: *Associates are trained on what to produce, but we don't describe how electrical and mechanical things work or why we produce in a certain way. Many of our current hires don't have much, if any, mechanical assembly experience.*

Early in that year, Steve launched training sessions teaching new associates not just how to wire a motor but also how a motor works and why we wire it the way we do, how a reducer works, and how to assemble and install one. In the end, when that associate is back on the line tightening bolts with a torque wrench, they should know why a pulley operation, for instance, needs a particular bolt-tightening sequence. And we hope they also know that the company is investing in their future growth.

Step four on the A3 is the team's list of what it intends to do and how. This is fairly straightforward and shown in the illustration, so I will not list each action here. I will draw your attention to the fifth item on the list, however, as this is directly related to the key task monitor: *Establish different levels of training matching production levels* was a project that we expected would take several months to finish, so a level-one KTM was created to help us create a plan and then track how we were performing against the plan.

A level-one KTM usually shows the project tasks cascading out over the year (*see page 122*). A level-two KTM offers more detail and shows all the work sequenced over about three months. A level-three KTM shows what an area such as new-product development is doing in a week, day by day, to satisfy a bigger KTM. A level-three KTM is often just written on a convenient whiteboard. In all cases, the main purpose of a KTM is to monitor the progress of a big project's work elements.

The left column of the KTM describes each step in the process. Every step has a time frame for expected execution shown to the right. The first three items on the KTM for manufacturing readiness—all critical to laying the groundwork for training— needed to be completed in the project's first month, so each item got a blue bar in January. Glancing at this sheet, we can see how the blue "plan" bars cascade across the year, showing when Steve intended to complete each step. Under the blue bars are blank boxes, waiting for another colored bar: green for accomplished, red for being off plan, and black for a delay in the plan.

The layout for KTMs is helpful in several ways. It breaks big projects into easier chunks. Anyone can see exactly what Steve and Adam have planned for this important project for the next several months. And we can tell at a glance whether the plan is moving ahead on schedule, as well as whether it is being updated or forgotten.

Level-one Key Task Monitor

Level 1	Stretch Innovation KTM (Key Task Monitor)																			
Project Started : Proposal Produced :		Project Description:												Project Leader :						
Key Activity	Week no.	4Q07 52	1st Quarter 5 / 9 / 13			2nd Quarter 18 / 22 / 26			3rd Quarter 31 / 35 / 39			4th Quarter 44 / 48 / 52			Improvem't Metric	Resp'y	Completion Date	
	Month	Dec	Jan / Feb / Mar			Apr / May / Jun			Jul / Aug / Sep			Oct / Nov / Dec					Plan	Actual
1																	Week 52	
2																	Week 18	
3																	Week 35	
4																	Week 35	
5																	Week 35	
6																	Week 39	
7																	Week 48	
8																	Week 39	
9																	Week 44	
10																	Week 52	
11																		
12																		

Comments

Key:
Plan
Actual
Off Plan

Checking the progress of improvement projects is part of my standardized work. Every Tuesday at 2 p.m., I begin a two-hour walk-around review of half of Lantech's WAR boards, looking specifically at the right side of the board for status of improvement projects. The KTMs tell me whether the project is progressing as planned and the intended next steps, as well as whether there are barriers that need my attention. I invite a rotating cast of managers on these two-hour tours, which gives me an opportunity to do some leadership coaching, as well as ensuring that the projects benefit from many points of view.

Just as I have time set aside every week to check on the progress of improvements, team leaders have time set aside every day to make progress on their projects. In general, production-line team leaders spend the first two hours of a day setting up for the work ahead, meeting with their teams, and then reporting upward regarding their needs. They spend another hour at the end of the shift setting up for the next day. Another hour or two might be spent chasing down an andon and halting process deterioration. Let's say this leaves two hours in a day for improvement work.

This time might be spent on tasks for a mission-critical project or a more run-of-the-mill improvement, such as reducing the number of defects in a troublesome process. A team leader might even use the time to work on something that is more of an adjustment—such as reconfiguring a work cell to accommodate a new takt time—than a true improvement. The important point is that they have time set aside for project work.

In the Netherlands, where both the workforce and the products are very stable, team leaders have been using their improvement time to create more intuitive workstations and more effectively standardize the work. Nearly every day, team leaders have had time for projects, so they created poka yokes to make wiring harnesses come together in a snap and have reduced setup time between different models. As demand for case erectors grew, they created new workflows that allowed everyone in the work cells to more smoothly adjust as takt times changed.

In 2015 and 2016, we went from making eight case erectors every week to making 12 in our Cuijk facility without adding any employees. That is 50% more machines we can ship without additional labor costs every week.

And in Louisville, where personnel in offices such as engineering, finance, sales, and procurement are also very stable, managers used the improvement tools—the A3 and KTMs—to manage the work of integrating a whole new business.

The origin of this new business, once again, has its roots in the Great Recession, when I began signing every check and questioning costs. I discovered that we were buying lots of fairly simple parts and paying more than we should in order to get small quantities shipped to us frequently—the same faux just-in-time production that we discussed earlier. I seized the opportunity to buy one of those suppliers and simply moved its machines into a corner of our facility, hired a few of its people, and looped its production into our kanban system. That worked so well that we started to look at how we might expand on the idea.

In 2013, a building that was about 50 yards off our loading dock came up for sale, and I jumped at it, imagining all of the insourcing we could accomplish in a space that size. It was a big project to manage. The facility needed to be remodeled for our uses. We needed to buy a laser cutter, brake presses, and other new-to-us tooling, hire new associates, and map out how the new parts would fit into production schedules. I was determined to do it all in-house.

This was a very large project, creating a new business category. At Toyota, it might have been called *kaikaku*, meaning a revolutionary change in the business rather than incremental improvements. To manage it, we reached for the same tools we were using for improvement projects because they kept the details on public display instead of hidden away on someone's hard drive and because we could use the habits of the daily management system to drive the work forward.

We kept track of all the deadlines and different bits of work with a series of A3s and KTMs. Jack Kelley, our controller, had an A3 on his improvement board for the insourcing project and different levels of KTMs that kept us on track with the facility work every step of the way. Anyone looking at the board could see the dates on which each piece of equipment was due to arrive, when new electrical systems were being run to support that equipment, and when we intended to start hiring and training new associates to run those machines.

During the height of activity on the new facility, which we all refer to as "Decimal" because the building's official address is on Decimal Drive, we were meeting for 10 minutes every morning in front of Jack's improvement board. Being able to discuss the daily and weekly deadlines and progress by glancing over KTMs made those meetings both fast and productive.

We do not have enough experience buying new facilities and launching new businesses to offer comparative results. But I can say that we bought the Decimal building in September 2013 and we were making parts in time to production needs in January 2014. Four months to launch that new business seemed reasonable to me.

For all the success of improvement work in Louisville administration and Cuijk production, however, we still had challenges. Bob was certainly right that, without stability, improvements would not materialize or stick. We thought that processes in the Louisville factories were stable enough to begin improvements. But the improvement work we tried to do initially did little more than reveal instabilities due to time-consuming employee turnover and the necessary distraction of new-product integration.

Once we realized that production team leaders just didn't have time for improvements in Louisville, we took a step back and used A3s and KTMs to try to address root causes of that instability (resulting in the training project outlined at the beginning of this chapter). As of this writing, team leaders are still using improvement time to train new employees, shuffle people around to fill gaps and cross-train, or plan for new product upgrades or modules. That work has been necessary and fruitful. Still, we look forward to the day when we have *maintained* the Louisville operations well enough to move on to improvement at a higher rate like our team in Cuijk.

Chapter 10

Strategy Planning and Deployment

ack in the day when we would have really high-level annual
strategic planning sessions, my lake house saw lots of action.
Every year I would gather our top seven or eight executives,
along with a hired facilitator, and spend a few days visioning and
jockeying for position.

We might do a game or a personality test to break the ice,
then some visualization exercises to limber up. We would break
into teams for SWOT[24] analysis of Lantech's market position, or
we might try to broaden our minds with the most current business-
school theories. After the *Harvard Business Review* published a
piece on the "Blue Ocean Strategy" about finding new market
spaces and creating demand instead of meeting it, for instance, we
spent a good bit of time trying to find a big blue ocean in that lake
outside the windows.

Then we would take this wisdom and our newfound understanding and apply them to Lantech's goals and situation to come
up with a list of really important projects. There would be another
round of jockeying, some politely worded finger-pointing, and a
few reminders about our real aims, and then we would whittle and

---

24. SWOT: strength, weakness, opportunity, and threat. This is usually a simple four-
quadrant graph used to evaluate an idea, product, or market sector.

winnow until we had about eight solid projects intended to help us meet our strategic goals. These would be big projects with global reach or engineering fixes that required retooling and retraining throughout a product line. All were of existential importance.

Back in Louisville, we would roll out the big plan to midlevel managers. To manage our resources and create accountability, we used the X-Matrix that we learned from consultants who had worked in Toyota Group suppliers. We explained to managers what they were going to do and, maybe, how they should do it, but we rarely concerned ourselves with when they might do this work.

From this process, we got pretty consistent results. The top two projects in our carefully ordered list generally got completed satisfactorily. Progress on the other six languished and stuttered. After 90 days, a project might lose resources through reassignment, or the world would change on us and it would no longer seem that emerging markets were desperately in need of that machine that seemed so great at the lake house. Most years we went back to the lake house in the late winter or early spring and tried to retune or reboot plans that had wandered off course or failed.

I told Bob Morgan about this pattern of 75% project failure, and he asked me about the process. I told him about the trips to the lake house, the top eight executives, the visioning exercises, and the X-matrix. He listened to all of it, nodding thoughtfully.

Now remember this is the guy who told me he would help us at Lantech only if the top executives agreed to spend weeks in the operations work cells, learning processes and rewriting standard work. This is the man who put me on the paint line and told me it was time for me to start teaching workshops. Knowing all of this, I should have been prepared for his answer, which was simply, "You're too far from the work."

The most important step in getting where you want to go is knowing where you start from, Bob reminded me. An engineering team cannot successfully design a machine for a market segment that they know little about. In the same way, leaders cannot design a business plan without knowing all the facts. And by "knowing all the facts" I mean actually going out and collecting all the facts—not leading with assumptions or relying on the presentations of department heads.

For instance, if I was trying to make my son, Jimmy, into an NBA player, I could brainstorm a really great plan to get us there. I could hire the best coaches and have Jimmy work on his jump shot for hours every day and practice free throws and layups until he was exhausted. But what if we overlooked the fact that he never learned to dribble the ball and—if genetics has anything to say about it—Jimmy will probably not grow much taller than 6 feet? Instead of making an NBA player, I would have demoralized a fine boy simply because I did not know or overlooked important facts.

Without granular information about the real issues facing a business, there's a good chance that any plan will be based on incorrect assumptions and will not just fail but become counter-productive. But how do we make sure that a handful of top executives have all of the necessary information to make strategic plans? We start by inviting a lot more people to the table.

That first year that I sought help with strategic planning, Bob asked me what Lantech's most pressing problem was, and I vented my frustration over the deterioration of improvement work. If you remember, I had completely reworked the paint line into a synchronized system, only to have the system fall apart as soon as I left for Europe.

Since Bob and I were already talking about implementing a daily management system (this was 2007), we agreed to use his ideas about strategic planning and deployment to launch the system as a strategic initiative. The two systems worked hand in glove, encouraging associates and executives throughout the company to adopt some of the same daily and weekly habits.

Over the years since that first strategic deployment, we have refined some of our processes for the better, so let's look at a more recent project for a good example of what we do and why. Like all strategic projects, this one began with a problem or an opportunity that became apparent over the course of several months. We do not pull a lot of data or do fancy calculations when deciding where to focus strategic planning because the areas in need are generally obvious. Instead, our projects are the result of weeks and months worth of conversations among managers and executives about how we're doing and where we are going.

Some of these conversations are informal. Others are part of a highly structured process of quarterly reflections, which I will discuss in a moment. For now, I can report that by September of every year, I am well versed on what worked and did not in the prior year's strategic deployments. I add this information to the mental hopper, along with knowledge of the international markets, economic trends, and ideas or concerns I have heard from customers and our folks in sales and operations. We then define the five to eight big subjects that we need to address to keep Lantech healthy and growing. My lake house is no longer part of the process.

In 2012, international markets were on my mind. India, Brazil, and China had all been encouraging industrialization for a number of years, and it was clear that a much larger middle class was emerging in those countries. Working, prosperous families want toilet paper, canned beverages, diapers, and all manner of goods that need to be manufactured, packaged, and shipped. New factories in those countries needed to secure their loads with stretch wrap.

The question was, how prepared were we in Kentucky to meet international demand? To help answer that question, one of the strategy-planning teams that year was international markets, tasked with investigating our global capabilities.

When we begin the strategic planning and deployment cycle, we start with senior leadership deciding on the makeup of five-person teams. Team membership is seen as a training and mentoring opportunity, so we look for up-and-comers on staff as well as subject matter experts and people who are well versed in the process of strategic deployment. Invitations for team membership are generally extended in September.

In October, we gather our entire management staff of about 25 people to introduce the year's strategic subjects and teams and do a structured, standardized reflection on the last round of strategy deployment. Our reflection process is stolen straight from the US military's after-action review. First, we reiterate what the plan was. Then we describe what actually happened. We talk about what worked and then what did not work. We make lists of what experiences we would like to repeat or incorporate into our process and—from the did-not-work category—what we will not do again.

We usually pick a theme for the year, too, like classic rock or Disney movies; people choose team names, illustrations, and such based on their name. Some team members even dress in costume for report outs. In addition to the fun, we always hold a workshop to teach everyone the what and why of the characterization process, which is the teams' next task. Management staffs that are not assigned to a team are usually assigned to support certain projects or mentor teams.

Directly following this process of reflection and selection, we move to characterization, which is step two of strategic planning. Characterization can be thought of as another term for "go see." This is where we send people out to investigate the current condition, encouraging them to keep their hands in their pockets and their lips zipped and really look at the work. We ask our people to become neutral observers, uncovering the facts without bias. It is a little like having embedded reporters fan out through the company, and I have found these reports to be far more valuable than asking department heads for presentations on the effectiveness and efficiency of their own areas. Those reports are too vulnerable to ego and self-interest, no matter how honest the leader is trying to be.

So, we ask our unbiased observers to look at how people, paper, and parts flow through any process. We use "people, paper, and parts" to help teams remember what they are looking at, but you could also call it "people, information, and material or product flows." This is the three-legged stool involved in every bit of work—even accounting and sales and on-site service—and we want to make sure our people are looking hard at how the elements move and interact.

As far as I am concerned, this is the real work of strategy. Too often, strategy is treated as some intellectual exercise—an ivory-tower pastime without any threat of dirty fingernails. Bob taught us that strategic thinking must begin within the real work of the company and that it is a marriage of the current condition and the future vision. Every opportunity must be connected in some way with the present. For instance, I would not have suggested international markets as a topic for strategic planning if we were not already selling machines abroad.

After people look hard at the process, we ask them to work in their teams to digest the information and then sketch or characterize it. These sketches are more creative and opinionated than simple reporting. Think of the cartoon portraits you see quickly sketched by artists in a tourist town or theme park. The artist emphasizes one feature or another for comic effect.

After weeks of investigating the current condition, we draw pictures that emphasize the most important facts. This characterization phase typically lasts 4–6 weeks, and we gather for the report out either just before or after the Thanksgiving holiday.

In 2012, members of the international markets team took a day out of their usual jobs every week and dived deep into the current condition. They pulled data on calls to the customer support lines, interviewed foreign customers and distributors on the telephone and by e-mail, and sat with customer support associates while they took calls. Team members met in their designated team area at least once a week to review progress and make plans. They also received regular visits from senior leaders or managers mentoring the team and keeping the process on track.

When the characterizations were complete, the whole management group gathered again in a big room we call the Learning Center. Teams posted results and drawings on grease boards and flip-chart paper all around the room. Most of the year, this room—windows included—is covered in paper charts and hand-drawn pictures.

It did not surprise me when the international markets team reported that Lantech was just about impossible to do business with from India, Brazil, or China. We were unavailable by phone during working hours for much of the world. Questions could get answered by e-mail, but the time difference and translation issues meant distributors and customers might wait days for simple answers. It is fair to say that our efforts lacked urgency.

Actual support was centralized in either Louisville or Cuijk. Since European and Indian safety requirements are different from the US rules—even Canadian requirements are different—some of our parts did not conform to international requirements and needed to be substituted. Our operating manuals were in English only. Some of our measurements were not translated to metric. And if they wanted parts shipped, people had to fill out multipage forms demanding arcane information. We seemed like yokels who had never shipped overseas before. The cartoon drawing this team made showed a frustrated customer with a telephone pressed to their ear, listening to a recording that Lantech was closed for the day. But the problem was much bigger.

By this time, Gina and I had learned the value of keeping close tabs on the characterization teams. Not only do we want to make sure they are digging deep and staying on track, but we also want to know what they are finding out. This way, we know what they will be presenting at the characterization report out and we can be ready to break people into new teams to begin working on solutions.

When the report presentations are completed we began a discussion of what the potential solutions might be, consistent with our company priorities, at a meeting of the entire management team. In 2013, the international markets team made a number of suggestions for projects:

1. Create an international shipping coordinator job to handle all overseas shipping. (sales and shipping)

2. Implement standard global communication and systems to speed response time. (IT)

3. Cross-train to support international parts. (tech services)

4. Simplify and standardize all technical language to ease translations. (tech services)

5. Focus on attracting bilingual associates, especially Spanish-speaking technicians. (HR)

6. Create web sites in other languages; convert measurements to the metric system. (marketing)

No final decisions on projects are ever made at this meeting because we need a couple of weeks to shake the trees. In fact, the two weeks following the characterization reports have proved crucial to our success. This is when managers from throughout the company bring their teams into the Learning Center to review the characterizations and ask, "What can we do to attack these problems, consistent with our priorities." Most of our solutions come from this kind of departmental entrepreneurialism.

A team from product development might look at the board and realize that the new series of stretch wrappers under development need to be designed in metric as well as English units and that they need to incorporate all international safety standards. The sales team begins discussing how to present Lantech better in China. Another team from tech services, meanwhile, decides to create a plan to provide 24/7 telephone support.

Some of the projects—usually two or three a year—involve cross-functional coordination and require broad high-level sponsorship. The majority of our solutions, however, are as simple as teams of people looking at a list of what we really need and saying, "Hey, we can do that. Or, you know what would be really cool too?"

Sometime in December or early January comes step three: creating and assigning projects, writing the A3s and KTMs that will guide teams through the coming months. This project selection phase, remember, used to take three days, eight executives, and a lake house. It now requires about three months, up to 30 people, and a lot of looking and sketching and paper. The bigger difference is that now these projects are relevant and get done.

Once the A3s are written—whether in the Learning Center, within a team assignment, or in a department—they are all hung on the right side of the WAR boards. I review progress on half of A3s on Tuesdays and the other half the following Tuesday. That means every A3 is fully updated and ready for CEO review at least twice a month, and that has helped speed our progress too.

Remember the annual reflection process, based on the US military's after-action reviews? We do those on a quarterly basis, as well. We pull the full management team back into a meeting every three months and look at the progress of every strategic A3. Projects are displayed as to the risk of being completed on schedule and are shown as red, yellow, or green. Red and yellow projects get the most attention. When a project is struggling, we ask for ideas as to how to move it forward. We celebrate the completed projects with a final reflection.

A few pages ago I listed preliminary improvement projects proposed by the international markets group. It was not a bad list. But look at what the team actually did, after some tree shaking and reflection, to improve our standing in the global marketplace:

1. Tech services created 24/7 telephone customer support without adding new staff. Instead, they experimented with and perfected scheduling for associates that leaves one person on call every night, on a rotating basis. The on-call associate usually fields two or three calls a night—all taken at home. Occasionally a customer will need a part right away and the associate might make a midnight run into the office to grab a part and run it over to the airport for shipment. The upside is associates get more flexible scheduling during the week. And Lantech is always open.

2. The operational manuals department spearheaded a company-wide shift to standardized terminology and simplified technical English for all communications, enabling easier, less expensive translations for both technical and marketing materials.

3. After doing a thorough review of our visibility and potential in China, the sales department was instrumental in creating a new subsidiary in Beijing to sell Lantech products. Sales also pushed for Lantech brochures to be translated into several languages, using the new standardized terminology.

4. The G-Series of stretch-wrap machines, launched that year, was compliant with all international safety standards. It was designed to be built with either SAE or metric steel, so that we could build it overseas, as well.

There are probably a hundred reasons that Lantech makes a lot more money than we used to. But this is a major factor: we can now execute on good ideas across the company. During those meetings in the Learning Center, I am sitting down with all layers of management, talking about what is important, about our threats and opportunities, and then asking for their best ideas. Completing the projects that come out of those meetings is hard-wired into everyone's schedules, just as mentoring and pushing projects forward are hardwired into mine.

Managers make better independent decisions now because they have a broader view of the company and its aims. They sit in strategic planning sessions and discuss a variety of ideas from many vantage points, learning the risks and rewards of everything from international trade to new product launches.

This strategy deployment process, married with the daily management system, is also the reason that we are now able to launch new products that are stable within six months. Some of these products are completely new ideas, never attempted in our industry, and they are being shipped error-free within half a year.

Considering the fact that Lantech's life blood has always been innovation, that means we are creating a more stable future for this company—and maybe for my son, Jimmy, if that NBA career fails to pan out.

In fact, let's go to a new product and see how the management system guides it from idea to launch in order to see the big picture.

Chapter 11

Solving the Future

People like to think of new-product development as rooted in wild creativity. It's a romantic idea—that innovation hits like a bolt of genius electricity and if we just wait patiently and have smart, receptive people on staff, innovation will come. Certainly that can happen. But for us, great ideas are usually rooted in painstaking problem solving, and it feels less like a bolt from the blue than a smack on the forehead and a resounding "Duh."

This is not to say that our solutions are not creative. It is just that they do not come from the clear blue sky. All of them are deeply rooted in the lessons we have learned from Bob Morgan and other lean masters: seeing clearly without prejudgment, listening to what the customer is saying and *not* saying, and trusting the process.

I say *the* process because it turns out there really is just one. We used to think of the kaizen blitz as something entirely different from 3P[25] and apart from the high-level work of hoshin planning. But it turns out that improvement, new-product development, and strategic deployment are connected to and governed by the daily management system we have developed.

---

25. "Production preparation planning," which is a common term for lean product and process development.

The best example of this at Lantech can be seen in the process of creating the L-Series line of automatic stretch wrappers, in which a really innovative product line was born of dogged determination, sand castle maintenance, and a few regular daily habits. In fact, the product is so much a part of our management and operating system that we called the breakthrough LeanWrap technologies.

Some years back, during the Great Recession when we had extra people in new-product development and time to think due to a relaxed production schedule, we began focusing on a bigger idea than just the physical wrapping of loads for shipment. Instead, we started to think about loss. Every year, millions of products are lost due to damage in transit. It is a waste of resources, materials, and money. It means unnecessary additions to landfill and pollution globally.

On what scale is this problem? After some digging we found a study that estimated total loss in the US food and beverage sector due to expiration and damage in shipment to average around 1% of total sales annually.[26] In 2007, that loss was $15 billion. Let's say that loss due to transportation damage alone was at least half of the 1%, or $7.5 billion in food and beverage.

Next, we expanded our field to include all goods shipped worldwide. After all, few of our customers trade in the United States only. Gross world product was just below $80 trillion in 2014,[27] so we were confident in saying that every year, multiple billions of dollars in goods are lost to damage in transit worldwide. We decided not to quibble about whether that loss equaled

---

26. Joint Industry Unsaleables Leadership Team, "2008 Joint Industries Unsaleables Report," Grocery Manufacturers Association and Deloitte Consulting LLP (2008).
27. Gross world product is the combined gross national products of each country in the world. "Gross world product," https://en.wikipedia.org/wiki/Gross_world_product, last updated March 1, 2016..

$40 billion or $60 billion. In human terms, the value of loss due to damaged shipments is roughly equal to the entire GDP of Lithuania or Nepal.

By this time, we also knew that by simply looking at a problem, setting standards, and using the daily management process, we could see at least 50% improvement in 12 months. And then we could knock it down by half again, just by watching and fixing. The possibility of attacking a serious global problem was intoxicating. Imagine the value we could help return to the global economy while growing Lantech.

We began, of course, with our own customers. We knew there were problems out there; we heard the stories. One big food manufacturer had an entire tractor-trailer's worth of goods returned by a big-box retailer more than once due to damage to poorly wrapped goods between the supplier and the customer. A dockworker opened up the trailer, saw a toppled load, and simply closed the doors and sent it back. Our customer then lost its prime shelf location in the store in favor of the retailer's own in-house brand.

In another case that I saw at 2 a.m. in the parking lot of a Pennsylvania grocery store, a load of pineapple had arrived completely toppled. There were pineapples all over the truck. In that case, the store manager called in extra help to unload the truck by hand. More temporary workers were called in to cut up the damaged fruit, and the store manager held a sale on precut pineapple that week. Certainly, losses were suffered. But by whom?

Neither retailers nor manufacturers tracked transport damage because money changes hands. Most retailers get a 1% discount on goods from manufacturers to cover damage in shipment. These common agreements are the reason that retailers accept some damage without complaint and rely on the occasional sale on precut pineapple to balance things out. Consequently, manufacturers rarely hear about damage in transit and cannot report numbers back to us. Beyond anecdotes, we had no data on scale or specifics regarding damage.

That lack of attention to the problem was starting to change. Poorly wrapped loads were becoming more hazardous due to another big trend in the marketplace: green packaging. Consumers wanted final products to contain less material bound for the landfill. They were tired of fighting through plastic clamshells and multiple layers to get to the product. Even individual water bottles were changing, with skins so thin they were more like water balloons. When loads toppled, it was a much bigger loss.

I have said that the real creativity of problem solving usually involves just figuring out how to actually see the problem, and that was certainly true in this case. How do you see into an under-reported problem that originates in another company's operations? Really, we need to be in the middle of the action. So, we asked two of our biggest customers whether we could come in and run our machines at the ends of a couple of their production lines. They took one look at our offer of free expert labor and said, yes, of course.

For about six months, we wrapped every load that came off those production lines. Then we put people on roads, rails, and airways to meet trucks at their final destinations and inspect the loads. What we discovered confirmed our suspicions: loads that were correctly wrapped by well-maintained machines had no trouble in transit. The trick was wrapping every load correctly on every shift.

There's a science to creating a high-quality wrap as economically as possible—a balance of containment force and material usage, a strong grip on the pallet without dangling ends of film— and it can be thrown out of balance fairly easily. A new brand of stretch film or a forklift colliding with a camera sensor, for example, could change the settings just enough that wrapped loads *looked good* but were weakened.

With our experienced engineers on the case even the occasional complaints about damage ceased. Stretch-wrap machines ran consistently. Our engineers even started helping solve problems on upstream operations. Six months in, factory managers at our client sites noticed a difference. Both customers asked us to expand our "program" to all the other lines in their factory. Using our own employees to run every machine full-time was not economically feasible—not when we're trying to correct a global issue—but the experience sent us traveling down two paths.

First, we started a new A3 in our annual strategy deployment session in 2012—a super A3 that spawned several more sub-A3s and key task monitors, all of which were problem solving our way toward creating a new service product. We hired a manager, Alex Verret (from chapter 7), and used those A3s and KTMs to explore ideas and carry questions to different departments.

From the beginning, we realized that flying our engineers to customer sites and charging $125 an hour to set standards and teach good practices did not make sense long term. Customers would focus on limiting time with our engineers to save money instead of keeping load quality as a goal. So, we needed to hire and train local service technicians to work in specific regions and create maintenance routes among customers. We envisioned a subscription service for high-quality loads, where local technicians would go into customer sites, set up and maintain machines, and create good processes like we do in our factories: remove waste from the process, create standardized work, and maintain the sand castle on a regular basis.

We found that it usually takes a week of daily visits to set the standard and get it running consistently. After the customer is producing all high-quality loads, we keep coming back once a week because, in the field just like in our own operations, we use the rule of five: every newly implemented solution is observed by a team leader for its next five cycles in order to catch any problems. We added Internet-based communications to the machines as well—the project that Jeff Collins took on in chapter 7—so our technicians would receive a text whenever a stretch wrapper perceived it was running outside of specifications. In this way, even when our technicians have cut back maintenance visits to once a month, we have a window into load quality at all times.

While Alex was experimenting with the service offering, we also thought about the factories we could not touch with a subscription service. Our goal, after all, was worldwide reduction in transportation damage. At least we could take the lessons we learned from our experiment and teach others, we thought.

So we created the "10-Step Process for Damage Reduction through More Effective Stretch Wrapping" (*see right*). We put the steps on poster boards and unveiled them at the biggest packaging equipment trade show of 2012. People were very interested as they read the steps. We thought it was helpful. But it was just words.

At the next year's 2013 convention in Las Vegas, as we proudly set up our posters again, a major bottler pulled my dad aside and said kindly, "Nobody's going to do that."

He was right. We had "fixed" the problem by trying to push some pretty hard and tedious work downstream, and that just does not work. We have been at the end of production lines long enough to know the pressures people face there. Everyone has production targets (e.g., number of wrapped pallet loads out the door), and everyone faces trouble when those targets are missed. Learning and maintaining the proper containment force on a stretch-wrapped load were difficult and not priorities.

10-Step Process for Damage Reduction through More Effective Stretch Wrapping

Getting Started

1. Adopt a containment force as the critical specification for damage reduction.
2. Suggest starting with Lantech recommended containment force to establish the wrapping standard.
3. Evaluate "current condition" including containment force, effective load bind to pallet, and film tails.

Maintain the Process

4. Establish the required revolutions of film at a realistic and sustainable wrap force to establish desired containment force on the load. Do not just turn up wrap force to a level that may result in unacceptable film breaks.
5. Confirm that at least the recommended containment force is everywhere on the load.
6. Avoid reducing gage and/or increasing pre-stretch without considering the impact on sustainable wrap force and resulting in containment force.

Wrap a "Safe" Load

7. Establish a wrapping standard to include recommended containment force, effectively bonded load to pallet, and no film tails.
8. Add all machine settings and film choices required to maintain the desired containment force into the wrapping standard.
9. Measure containment force frequently.
10. Establish timely process for reacting to any discovered variance from wrapping standard.

My dad and I were leaning against a railing at the end of a long day in Las Vegas, looking over the convention floor, having a beer, and talking about what the bottler said. Now, I have great respect for my dad. He founded not only Lantech, but also the entire stretch-wrap industry for shipping.

When he handed me the reins of this company in the mid-1990s, he was perfectly happy to "retire" to new-product development, where he remains our guru in chief. Even if I am occasionally hectored for additional resources at holiday meals—"Please pass the rice and I need more engineers"—my dad remains one of Lantech's most valuable resources. So when he got that little light in his eye, I knew we were heading down a new path.

Our problem, he pointed out, was that we were making good loads hard to get. Making an effectively wrapped pallet should be as simple and intuitive as letting your hand fall naturally on the next piece of work.

It was a great dream. But when one pallet has 60 cases of toilet paper and the next one to be stretch wrapped has 40 cases of heavy dishwashing soap, requiring different compressions and wrap patterns, a hard-pressed operator has to make a bunch of choices grounded in the realities of what happens in the dark and shaky box that is the back of a tractor trailer. It's little wonder that machine settings were often suboptimal.

For a couple of years, we had been experimenting with touch-screen technology, just to keep pace with the modern world. Now, what if that hard-pressed operator could tap a screen indicating what the load looked like and let the stretch wrapper do the calculation? That would make sense. The screen could even have a picture of the product or pictures indicating that the load was light, heavy, or mixed. The operator would tap a series of pictures to describe the load and let the machine do the rest.

From that convention hall, my dad came back to Kentucky, grabbed a couple of engineers, and built a prototype, answering the very basic questions about whether certain algorithms would work. Then the idea went to our end-of-year strategic planning session and was vetted by the entire management staff. We started calling the project Load Guardian, and an A3 was written (*see page 148*).

Take a look at item 4, *How to Investigate and Get This Done*. This is an early draft of the key task monitors to come. The project leader, in consultation with others during strategic planning, created the list of tasks that needed to get completed over the following year to push a project forward. Then he put the tasks in sequence and cascaded them out over the year in order to create the level-one KTM. If we were creating a new product, for instance, the KTM might show that a working prototype is due at the end of March, parts need to be ordered for the next iteration by April 1, and assembly is expected to begin in late May.

A level-two KTM lists what needs to get done during the next three months to keep the project's level-one KTM on target. This looks like the level-one form with colored boxes, but it has even more detail, including a week-by-week task list. These KTMs are created just before a quarter begins so we can take into account what actually happened during the last quarter.

Finally, at the local level, a level-three KTM is often created on a grease board. In new product development, for instance, if a level-two KTM shows that this week is slated for prototype assembly, the board might show that we expect the film delivery system to be completed Wednesday, the base to be assembled Thursday, and the control panel to be installed and tested on Friday. In new product development—as in the marketing department— much of the daily work schedule is laid out on those level-three KTMs, since most of that department's work is project based.

Initial A3 for the Load Guardian Project

A-3 PROPOSED

PROJECT TITLE: LOAD GUARDIAN PHASE 1   PREPARED BY: RICHARD JOHNSON

---

1. BUSINESS ISSUE / NEED

Develop machine based control system that is result oriented instead of machine control oriented. A control system that is easier to understand and provides easier machine setup that will dramatically improve the load wrap quality and successful load shipments. This control system will provide key differentiation points when compared to competitive offerings and focus on the core reason for wrapping loads, "Containment force". Our competition is more focused on economy of wrap than quality of wrap.

2. DELIVERABLE / VALUE

An operator interface platform that guides the operator through machine setup based on expected results instead of setting machine functions through trial and error to achieve a successful wrap profile.

Intuitive screens with more graphic representation, easier to translate. Adopt symbols and screen layout similar to modern smart phone technology. Basic setup will utilize four screens to build the wrap profile, A. select load shape, B. Containment (light-heavy), C. Load fit to pallet, D. Overwrap. Advanced set up screens will be available for customization of wrap profile by the more experienced operators.

Containment force monitoring will be provided to ensure any changes made by the operator will not compromise the load containment force required to provide successful shipment.

Phase 1 will include – new screen interface, 1/2 layer resolution, containment force monitoring, profile management screens, advanced wrap profile editing.

3. CURRENT CONDITION

Load Guardian program developed and screens defined for basic and advanced operator interaction. Algorithms developed to control machine functions based on operator input of load characteristics.

Film testing to verify performance of film considering variables of film gauge, film type, % of payout and its effect on containment force. This data was used to develop film performance curves to aid in automatic machine setup.

WORK REQUEST

DATE: **1/14/15**   REV DATE: **4/10/15**   REV NUMBER:

---

4. HOW TO INVESTIGATE AND GET THIS DONE

Follow phase 1 deliverable document that identifies features and functions for phase 1 implementation

- Complete development to phase 1 specifications
- Complete alpha installations; 2 locations installed, 3 more installations desired. Working with marketing to identify.
- Collect feedback from alpha locations
- Identify cross function team for implementation into engineering and manufacturing
- Develop implementation A3's and KTM;s
- Follow implementation flow chart developed for software type implementations
- Develop QLM alpha based on AB platform
- Place QLM alpha at multiple customer locations to gain operation and performance learnings
- Review data collected from both alpha programs to identify iterations needed before production implementation
- Third alpha location selected, Conagra Indiana (2 – SLA machines)

---

5. FUTURE STATE

LG phase 1 implemented into engineering and mfg with updated machine manuals and TSG group associates trained.

---

6. VERIFICATION

SLA and QLA machines shipping with Load Guardian installed

Are management and maintenance tools in place?

149

Production, on the other hand, is 80%–90% customer fulfillment work and 10%–20% project work. Other departments such as technical services or customer service have some mix of customer-need fulfillment and project work. So the boards we review on our daily walk-around reviews—and my weekly improvement reviews—look very different from one department to the next. Since I am looking at every board twice a month, I get familiar with them pretty quick.

And that is how we create new products now: week in, week out, we follow the path set up in strategic deployment, using the methods of the daily management system. We just keep at it.

Load Guardian was not the only component that we developed for our LeanWrap L-Series machines. We also created something we called Metered Film Delivery that more precisely measured and applied the right amount of stretch film for every load. To help secure loads to pallets and cleanly break the film, we added Pallet Grip and the Load Seeking Clamp 4.0.

The first of the new L-Series machines were shipped in January 2016 and, at the time of this writing, have been in place for six months. That is not much time to get a complete assessment, and we still struggle with the fact that most customers do not track how loads fare in shipment.

One high-volume customer with L-Series machines in place for six months does perform random quality checks on wrapped loads and reports that, so far, there has not been a single load found to be out of spec. This customer, who asked not to be named, has also followed loads to their destinations on a regular basis and found no damage due to poor pallet wrapping. This is heartening news, but it is just one customer. As of this writing, I am still trying to figure out how we can consistently "go see" the arrival of loads wrapped with L-Series machines to assess whether we are reducing shipping loss the way we hope.

Even if we are only 50% or 70% better, our customers are happy because we have been able to make some very immediate cost improvements. Part of the selling point of the L-Series is that when loads are wrapped correctly each time using Metered Film Delivery, less film is used. Now, stretch film might be just $1 a pound. But when 40 loads are wrapped every hour in a high-volume plant running two shifts a day, that can add up to 160,000 loads per year. Customers have calculated savings at $10,000 per year in film alone, to say nothing of loss due to damage.

So, we are a little closer to our goal. More important, though, we are closer to the next goal—the one we have not even thought of yet—because we have a tested and proven system for pushing innovative thinking into reality. Power is in the process.

Chapter 12

Securing the Future

A casual reader might skim these stories of maintaining and stabilizing and assume that we have been working hard just to tread water. This could not be further from the truth. Learning how to maintain our processes has helped Lantech improve its processes sustainably and tackle big-leap strategic initiatives. As a result, we have become a very profitable company.

In fact, as of this writing in the summer of 2016, Lantech has just recorded its most profitable quarter ever. Over the past few years, our profitability trend line has been on a steady upward path, showing 25%–27% improvement each period. For a manufacturer of capital equipment in the United States, this is remarkable.

We did not do this by outsourcing to a cheap-labor country, pressuring our people to work harder and faster, or squeezing out the last drop of waste. We still have plenty of that, unfortunately. What we have even more of now are customers, old and new. (In the same way that halting deterioration in a production process saves cost, preventing the deterioration in a customer relationship by shipping on time with perfect quality keeps the customers we have as we look for more.) We have plenty of competitors worldwide, yet we have steadily grown our market share.

More than that, we have confidence that comes from accumulating value by piling up improvements that actually stay in place and hit the bottom line. Lantech's gross margin has increased substantially every year since 2010. This is not from expense reduction. Our gross margin improvement is almost all resource cost savings due to the fact that we are not chasing big problems every day. As one example, our technicians no longer spend time on a regular basis making adjustments on the belt drive for the film-delivery system because they tracked down root causes for the belt tracking too far left or right and fixed it. We still do daily problem solving, of course, but the majority of our processes are stable. And the value of that is massive.

Every business is full of uncertainty. Strange and bad things happen all the time. Yet most people continue to design work for normal days and best-case scenarios. Then it is the line manager's job to chase the mistakes and messes such processes create.

What I learned from Bob Morgan, and from doing this work for nearly a decade now, is that a good management system is designed to accommodate the strange and bad. It keeps leaders close to the work and to the customer, allowing for fast reactions to issues large and small, while using PDCA for problem solving. A good system does not depend on uncontrollable processes to remain unchanging. A robust management system acknowledges the existence of random, ceaseless variation and directs people to fix the problems that fly off of our brilliant processes every day.

I began work on this book intending to share the remarkable power of these few core principles. I hope every reader comes away remembering, at the very least, that kaizen on top of chaos will only equal more chaos. The more important question at hand, however, is how you might create a system of your own.

Proceeding on Your Own: A Daily Management Action Plan

Most of us need a wise teacher at our side to guide us. You probably will not have the benefit of the entirely unique Bob Morgan. He spends most of his time circumnavigating the globe in his sailboat and actively avoiding work. Who can blame him?

Also, you will not be able to send an executive team to Lantech on a discovery mission. We have shut down our tourism department. In fact, I would strongly recommend against going on tours. For all of those years that we allowed nearly nonstop tours through our facilities, what visitors really saw—what made an impression—was our clean and well-organized spaces. But 5S is one of the by-products of our work; it does not stabilize processes or improve margins. I do not believe that anyone—no matter how perceptive—can see what really creates success during a three-hour tour.

Prework

Find a teacher who understands the power of maintaining processes and knows how to construct a daily management system that can be customized for your business. As part of the process of finding a teacher, articulate your most pressing business problem. Ideally, the management team will share consensus on this.

Step 1: Go see

Go see the work and begin to learn for yourself how it is actually done. Make sure you are in an area that produces that most pressing business problem that you previously articulated. If lead time is your biggest issue, make sure you are looking at lead time. Do not let anyone tell you what is happening in your value-creating processes. Do not rely on reports. Go and watch.

Draw pictures. Ask respectful questions. Think about how to make life easier and safer for associates on the front line.

At Lantech, our biggest problems were that improvements did not stick and the quality that we were delivering to customers was not improving. Most of our managers' time was spent fighting the same problems as last week. Our confidence wavered; sales were not growing. Sure, we still enjoyed the benefits of our transition from batch manufacturing to flow in operations in the mid-1990s, but I saw clear signs we were sliding backward. I began this journey by observing work in a feeder line for the S-Auto machine, in a shop building electrical panels. It had been improved many times through the kaizen process but was still delivering less than perfect quality.

Your problems will surely be different from ours, but step one will be the same. Name the problem, find a source of the problem, and go watch how the work gets done. If you omit this step, you will end up with some pretty management boards and a new daily walking exercise, but will achieve only disappointing results. So, find someone else to attend all those useless meetings that fill your days and head to the front line.

While you are there, sitting or standing for hours, observing frontline workers in action, you might start wondering how we created a world in which we believe that managers do not need to understand the actual value-creating work of their organization. Too many managers specialize in creating scorecards, measuring employees, and attending meetings with other managers. The people who are really creating value, meanwhile, are often on their own and—in manufacturing, anyway—are not only doing their own jobs, but also trying to juggle the defects that have trickled down from other processes in other areas of the business.

While you are in that other person's workspace, practice empathy. Imagine how you would feel to have someone observing you at close quarters. Think about what it means to be a servant leader. Know that you probably do not have the best answers. Actually, in this phase you are more student than servant leader. You will certainly be looking at processes you do not fully understand. Ask open-ended questions when there is an opportunity, but mostly keep your mouth closed and your hands out of the work.

Step 2: Use your knowledge

Now become the leader of an improvement team and fix the work process you observed. I dug deep into the work of the paint line, created a new schedule for the work, and, I believed, set up the front line for continuing success. When it all fell apart, I discovered exactly how hard we make life for our frontline supervisors and managers.

In taking this hands-on leadership role, I discovered that our management system did not enable long-term sustainable improvement. After learning to see the work, then learning to see the holes in our management system, my senior team (now completely changed from the folks I started with) and I understood some essential flaws of our system that we never would have understood otherwise.

Step 3: Create a prototype daily management system

Gather your senior management team around a whiteboard and map the flow of value in your organization. Typically, value runs from sales to engineering (if there is customization) to purchasing to production to shipping to installation. A service organization, government entity, or hospital will flow differently, but it always begins with the customer's request and moves through your organization to fulfillment of that request.

Clarify your organizational chart, define key value streams, and calculate run rates for just a few key metrics in each one. Without objective and visible-to-all run rates, people will not know normal from abnormal. Only when we can clearly see the first sign of abnormal can we intervene quickly and effectively. Remember: keep metrics to a bare minimum at first. I recommend using just two per area until an urgent need makes you add more.

Next, design your daily walk-around reviews. Discuss what stops you will make, who should be there, and where the boards will be located. Make sure every stop is in the work and within sight of the people actually doing the work. Define three or four levels of review. The first is between frontline associates and their team leader, who collects information on the day's needs and challenges. Level two is at the first line of management, with the area manager collecting information from all team leaders. Level three is either all the departments in a function, such as engineering or sales, or—depending on the size of your business—all function heads.

Everyone needs to be clear that the dynamic of the organization is shifting to focus on maintaining processes and responding quickly to problems. The old red-is-bad, green-is-good standard no longer applies. A red card on a board, indicating that a run rate has fallen outside of the norm, is an opportunity to find and correct a problem. Red is opportunity. Green is sometimes camouflage.

Each area, department, and function should create its own WAR board. A strong hint that your organization is moving in the wrong direction will be if all the boards look exactly alike. The right board for each area is the one that speaks most clearly to the people in that area. Senior leaders will be going to these areas every day and will soon become accustomed to how people organize information.

Also, coach everyone to be wary of stagnation. Beyond a few simple constants, such as the fact that maintenance is on the left side of the board and improvement on the right, the boards should be personal and constantly changing and updated.

Step 4: Attitude adjustments

Are people in your organization comfortable giving bad news? Do they love digging into problems? If not, your two most useful tools for the coming transition will be enthusiasm and respect. And of those two, respect is by far the most important.

Senior leaders and midlevel managers all need to discuss how questions will be phrased, how and when to coach subordinates, and how everyone should respond to the color red. If you suspect this will be difficult for your team, run rehearsals. During those rehearsals, coach people on the most respectful ways to conduct a walk-around review. Make sure you are displaying the respect you are asking from them as you coach. This is where a lot of folks need a coach or sensei to help out.

As a group, define success. Is it making your numbers, showing all green on your board? Or is success finding and fixing the root cause of problems in order to stabilize the process? Discuss how that will look. Also, is there an expectation that fixes should work perfectly the first time? If that is true, there is a deep misunderstanding of PDCA in your organization. Nothing ever works the first time, in my experience. Everyone should expect to try and try again. Celebrate the effort as well as the solution.

Depending on your organization, the issues to reflect upon will vary, but two key questions are always the same. What are senior managers doing to enable good work at levels below? What are lower-level managers doing to inform their bosses about the help they need to do good work? In a robust daily management system, information flows up and support flows down. Plan for this.

Step 5: Double down on standardization

This goes for management as well as for work processes. We are accustomed to the idea of standard work for associates at the front line. We may not do a very good job of creating that standard work, but at least there is a tradition of it.

Now, you will be standardizing the work of management through the daily discipline and cadence of the walk-around review. This will require commitment and persistence. Many managers will start out believing—and even saying out loud—that this whole idea is a waste of time. The only solution to this is to keep at it, doggedly walking through the morning reviews and helping naysayers fix problems until one day, a manager turns to you and says they actually have more time in their day to improve their value-creating processes. Others will soon acknowledge they have extra time, as well, and less stress. This is how you know it is time to add improvement work to maintenance.

Step 6: Solve the immediate

The easiest problems to see and solve are the ones happening right in front of you. Solving today's problems also has a much bigger impact on quality, we found, than solving for last week or last month.

It is also true that it is easier to find problems in a frequently observed process. A process that goes unobserved usually deteriorates and throws off all kinds of misleading signs. This is why it was so important for us to gain visibility into our processes by way of those run rates. If you can see the defect as it occurs, you have a much better chance of preventing its recurrence.

Problem solving will also bring up some cultural issues. It is not just that people want to hide problems; some people also want to write down all the problems they see, categorize them, and have meetings to decide which are the most important. The only way to avoid this wasteful activity is to put people to work solving the most immediate problems they see. Not to parrot Homeland Security, but people need to know that if they see something, they say something. And then they need to dig in and fix it.

In the beginning, you will hear complaints that people feel like they are chasing down so many little problems they will never get to the "important" ones. Tell them that these are the important problems. Soon enough, people will start talking about the extra breathing room they have in their schedules, and that will be the time to tackle the big, tricky issues that might require data-crunching black belts.

Step 7: Maintain until stable

When people are tempted to declare victory over deterioration and move on, ask them to pause. Working to solve the immediate and maintain our processes is where we discovered the greatest benefit to the business. Do not rush this phase.

How stable do underlying processes need to be before they can support true improvement? That depends upon your business. But most of those run rates on the left side of the review boards should be legitimately green for months before moving to improvements. And then, get everyone ready for some fresh red. In most cases, improvements will cause processes to wobble, and those run rates will turn red again. But that's OK. The act of stabilizing the new process—keeping attention on it—is what helps to ensure the success of the improvement.

Step 8: Stabilize strategic planning

As I noted in chapter 10, Lantech was brilliant at strategic planning. We had eight big initiatives introduced every year and about two implemented, on average. The problem was exactly the same as with our other processes. We lacked the discipline of standard work. In fact, we were unable to tackle a full roster of strategic initiatives until we had standard work that made sense. Now we know to begin by understanding the current process. "Go see" is always the first step.

Standard work for strategic planning begins with clearly stating the current condition. Then the resources required and the constraints and possible conflicts between projects are also spelled out. Over the life of the initiative, we use the daily management system to support and push ahead the work. How we ever executed on initiatives without this information and regular support is beyond me.

Most CEOs I have known—and I have had hundreds come through Lantech—think that they should start with strategic vision and then focus on dramatic improvement events and then maybe someday, somehow, think about daily performance. This kind of thinking is backwards, but it is practically written into the CEO self-image. Chief executives are supposed to come back like Moses from the mountain every year with inscribed tablets of prophetic wisdom.

Actually, we need to lead a drive to stabilize daily performance before we can think about dramatic improvements and strategic initiatives. Those inscribed tablets? We are not going to find them on a distant mountaintop. Real wisdom—aka great strategic initiatives—will spring from the work itself.

Homework

I have respected many of those presidents and CEOs I have known over the years as smart and hardworking. Yet, I have always had a problem convincing CEOs of one simple thing: they need to take the time to go where value is actually created. They need to learn to see the work and to see how their management system utterly fails to support the daily work. They need to be vulnerable enough to their own employees to ask simple questions. I know exactly how hard that is.

So my most important advice, stated in step one above, is to screw up your courage, put aside your daily distractions, and walk out into the work to see how value is created at the front line.

Feel free to let me know how it goes. I no longer host Lantech tours, but I'm happy to hear in writing about your successes and—much more important—to learn from your problems. You can contact me at: **info@lean.org**

The system described here actually works, and I know you can do this if I did. You just need to get out of your comfort zone and learn to see the real work of management. And never underestimate the value of a really great case erector or stretch wrapper.

Acknowledgements

This journey of continuing to build a successful brand and organization at Lantech has been made possible by many people's hard work, advice and knowledge. There are too many individuals to name, but a few in particular who told stories for the book are Gina, Steve, Ryan and Alex, I thank you for your input. To those in Product Development and Marketing who took the time to read the book and give their feedback, I thank you. For all those that I haven't mentioned, thank you for your help in making this book possible. And for all those in the Lantech workforce thank you for your contributions and support in making this journey a successful one.

I have been very fortunate to learn from Anad Sharma and his company TBM in the 1990's about kaizen, one-piece flow, and waste elimination and all the possibilities they provide. Then starting in the mid-2000's, Bob Morgan has mentored me and many of the folks at Lantech on how to continue our lean journey. And finally, Lantech's 45-year focus on customer value through innovation which continues to inspire me, would not have been possible without the tenacity and support of its founder, my father Pat Lancaster.

About the Author

Jim Lancaster is CEO and owner of Lantech.com, LLC. Lantech is recognized as the leader in stretch wrap technology and innovation. The company has sales and manufacturing headquarters in Louisville, Kentucky, sales and manufacturing facilities in the Netherlands, sales and service operations in Australia, and sales offices in China. Lantech manufactures packaging and material handling machinery, including stretch wrappers, conveyors, and case-forming equipment. Products are sold worldwide through a distributor and partner network, and directly to large consumer goods companies, such as Procter & Gamble, Lever Brothers, Nestlé, Miller Brewing, and Pepsi. Annual gross sales exceed $130 million and the company employs more than 500 associates.

Before joining Lantech, Jim worked in the financial industry with Catalyst Energy in New York City. In 1990, Jim joined Lantech as a Sales Manager in the Customs Machinery Group. After several promotions, he became President/CEO in 1995.

Lantech was one of the earliest companies to implement the Toyota Lean Principles in the early 90's, as chronicled in *Lean Thinking* by James Womack and Dan Jones, the Harvard Business Review, and other publications. Jim has participated in the Lantech lean journey for the past 21 years and is now the lead executive driving lean throughout the organization.

Jim personally supports and advocates for Technical and Vocational education in Louisville, through his involvement and board Chairman position at Jefferson Community and Technical College and with many other educational related efforts.

Index

*f denotes illustrations